PRAYING
GOD'S WORD
DAY BY DAY

BETH MOORE

PRAYING GOD'S WORD DAY BY DAY

A Year of
DEVOTIONAL PRAYER

PUBLISHING GROUP

NASHVILLE, TENNESSEE

Praying God's Word, Day by Day:
A Year of Devotional Prayer
Copyright © 2006 by Beth Moore
All Rights Reserved

ISBN 0-8054-4420-3
ISBN 13: 978-0-8054-4420-9
B&H Publishing Group
Nashville, Tennessee

Unless otherwise noted, all Scriptures are from the
New International Version (NIV) copyright © 1973,
1978, 1984 by International Bible Society. Other ver-
sions include the King James Version (KJV) and the
New American Standard Bible (NASB), copyright ©
The Lockman Foundation, 1960, 1962, 1963, 1968,
1971, 1972, 1973, 1975, 1977, used by permission.

Printed in the U.S.A.

To my beloved friend

Mary Ann

I know of no one who extols the power
of praying Scripture more than you.
You are unspeakably dear to me.

I love you,
Beth

For though we live in the world, we do not wage war as the world does. The weapons we fight with are not the weapons of the world. On the contrary, they have divine power to demolish strongholds. We demolish arguments and every pretension that sets itself up against the knowledge of God, and we take captive every thought to make it obedient to Christ.

2 Corinthians 10:3–5

INTRODUCTION

This book is a result of my unquenchable desire to share one of the most effective
approaches to the liberated life in Christ that
God has ever taught me: praying Scripture to
overcome strongholds.

Actually, I didn't discover what a vital part
of my liberation this approach has been until
long after I had begun practicing it. I suddenly
realized it was no accident that I was finally set
free from some areas of bondage that had long
hindered the abundant, effective, Spirit-filled
life in me. After the failure of all my formu-
las, in my desperate search for freedom I cast
myself entirely upon God. He faithfully led
me to several deliberate practices that He knew
would work. Stunningly, in fact.

Many of us have expended unknown energy trying hard to topple these strongholds on
our own, but they won't fall, will they? That's
because they must be demolished. God has
handed us two sticks of dynamite with which

to demolish our strongholds: His Word and prayer. What is more powerful than two sticks of dynamite placed in separate locations? Two strapped together.

And that's what this book is all about: taking our primary sticks of dynamite—prayer and the Word—strapping them together, and igniting them with faith in what God says He can do.

What makes these two sticks of dynamite so powerfully effective when strapped together? Let's consider the stick of prayer first. Prayer keeps us in constant communion with God, which is the goal of our entire believing lives. Yes, God wants to bring us healing, but more than anything else, He wants us to know our Healer. His chief objective is to keep us connected entirely to Him.

Then what makes the *Word* such a powerful stick of dynamite to demolish strongholds? According to 2 Corinthians 10:3–5, our objectives are to cast down anything that exalts itself in our thought life and to take our thoughts captive to Christ. And we do this every time we choose to think Christ's thoughts about any situation or stronghold instead of Satan's or our own. What are Christ's thoughts? The Word of God revealed to us.

In praying Scripture, I not only find myself in intimate communication with God, but my mind is being retrained, or renewed (Rom. 12:2), to think *His* thoughts about my situation rather than mine. This approach has worked powerfully every time I've applied it. It takes belief, diligence, and time, but the effects are dramatically liberating and eternal.

I am a fellow sojourner with you. I have made so many mistakes and learned so many hard lessons. Please don't misunderstand my intention and think I'm suggesting my own formula here. With all my heart, I believe it is one of God's. This book is about Him and the divine weapons He's given us to demolish strongholds. It's far more His Word than mine, and we've got a written guarantee on His. It's time to start igniting some dynamite!

JANUARY

THE GIANT STEP IN THE WALK OF FAITH IS THE ONE WE TAKE WHEN WE DECIDE GOD NO LONGER IS A PART OF OUR LIVES. HE IS OUR LIFE.

My Father, I acknowledge that You are the Lord Almighty. You are the first and You are the last, and apart from You there is no other God. Make me witness to the fact that there is no other Rock but You. Enable me to say with full assurance, "I know not one" (Isa. 44:6, 8).

You are my Lord, my Holy One, my Creator, my King. You are the One who made a way through the sea, a path through mighty waters (Isa. 43:15–16).

You are the Lord my God. I desire to love You, listen to Your voice, and hold fast to You, for You, Lord, are my life (Deut. 30:20).

HE WHO IS UNCONVINCED OF GOD'S FORGIVING LOVE IS UNCONVINCED THAT HE IS MORE THAN A CONQUEROR.

Father God, You made my Savior's life a guilt offering for me (Isa. 53:10). His death was enough to handle my guilt.

Lord Jesus, help me to accept and internalize the fact that if God is for me, who can be against me? (Rom. 8:31). It is You, God, who justifies (Rom. 8:33). Who is he that condemns? Christ Jesus, who died—more than that, who was raised to life—is at Your right hand, O God, and is also interceding for me (Rom. 8:34).

In all these things I am more than a conqueror through You who love me, Sovereign Lord (Rom. 8:37).

PATIENCE TO WAIT DOES NOT COME FROM SUFFERING LONG FOR WHAT WE LACK BUT FROM SITTING LONG IN WHAT WE HAVE.

The Lord will do great things for me, and I will be filled with joy. I will sow in tears, then I will reap with songs of joy. If I go out weeping, Lord, carrying seed to sow, I will return with songs of joy, carrying sheaves with me (Ps. 126:3, 5–6).

Please help me be willing to sow the seed of Your Word and to water it with my tears, believing You in the midst of my pain. If I do, You will be faithful to fill me with joy again. You will faithfully bring a harvest forth from my life. My suffering will not be in vain.

You, the God of all grace, who called me to Your eternal glory in Christ, will restore me and make me strong, firm, and steadfast after I have suffered a little while (1 Pet. 5:10).

MY GOD IS HUGE AND MY GOD IS ABLE. IF I DON'T GET WHAT I ASK HIM FOR, I KNOW I'LL GET SOMETHING BIGGER.

You alone are the Lord. You made the heavens, even the highest heavens, and all their starry host, the earth and all that is on it, the seas and all that is in them. You give life to everything, and the multitudes of heaven worship You (Neh. 9:6).

The earth is Yours, O Lord, and everything in it—the world and all who live in it (Ps. 24:1). For You are a great God, the great King above all gods. In Your hands are the depths of the earth, and the mountain peaks belong to You. The sea is Yours, for You made it, and Your hands formed the dry land (Ps. 95:3–5). In Your hand is the life of every creature and the breath of all mankind (Job 12:10).

Nothing on Earth Compares to the Strength God Is Willing to Interject into Lives Caught in the Act of Believing.

Father, so often I feel like the boy's father who first exclaimed, "I do believe!" then in a flood of sincerity cried out, "Help me overcome my unbelief!" (Mark 9:24). Please help me overcome my own unbelief, Lord, so I can start taking You at Your Word.

I pray that the eyes of my heart may be enlightened in order that I may know the hope to which You have called me, the riches of Your glorious inheritance in the saints, and Your incomparably great power to us who believe! (Eph. 1:18–19).

As You did for the jailer who received salvation through the witness of Paul and Silas, fill me with joy when I choose to believe You (Acts 16:34).

WE ARE WISE TO REMIND ONE ANOTHER NEVER TO FORGET WHO WE ARE AND NEVER TO FORGET WHO WE'RE NOT.

Father, Your Word says You will break down stubborn pride and make the sky above the proud like iron and the ground beneath him like bronze (Lev. 26:19).

Lord, Your Word is drawing a vivid picture of the arrogant life. Prayers lifted to heaven will seem to hit a ceiling of iron, and life beneath the feet will be hard.

Help me to be humble before You, Lord, because the life of the proud will eventually and undoubtedly become very hard.

My Savior and Redeemer, help me to take Your yoke upon Me and learn from You, for You are gentle and humble in heart, and I will find rest for my soul (Matt. 11:29).

LIKE EVE, WE WANT TO FEEL SMART, BUT NOTHING IS MORE IGNORANT THAN CHOOSING MAN'S INTELLIGENCE OVER GOD'S.

Lord God, when You asked the woman in the Garden, "What is this you have done?" her response was, "The serpent deceived me, and I ate" (Gen. 3:13).

Just as Eve was deceived by the serpent's cunning, the minds of even those with a sincere and pure devotion to Christ can be led astray (2 Cor. 11:3).

Please help me always be aware that the enemy will be up to his old tricks. Even the devout believer can be led astray if not held continually on the path by Your Word and keenly aware of Satan's schemes. Help me not be deceived by the serpent's cunning.

GOD CAN DO WHAT HE SAYS HE CAN DO PRECISELY BECAUSE HE IS WHO HE SAYS HE IS.

Lord God, help me to trust in Your unfailing love. Cause my heart to rejoice in Your salvation. Help me to sing to You, Lord, for You have been good to me! (Ps. 13:5–6).

The earth is filled with Your love, O Lord! Teach me Your decrees (Ps. 119:64). May Your unfailing love be my comfort, according to Your promise to Your servant (Ps. 119:76).

O God, help me to meditate on Your unfailing love! (Ps. 48:9). Help me not to have the sin of unbelief after all You've done to tell me You love me, after all You've done, Lord, to demonstrate Your love for me.

WE NEED MORE THAN A LEADER
ON OUR ROAD TO FREEDOM.
WE NEED A SAVIOR,
ONE WHO KEEPS ON SAVING.

Lord Jesus, You came and preached peace to those of us who were far away and peace to those of us who were near. For through You, Jesus, we both have access to the Father by one Spirit.

Consequently, we are no longer foreigners and aliens but fellow citizens with God's people and members of His household, built on the foundation of the apostles and prophets, with You, Christ Jesus, Yourself as the chief cornerstone.

In You the whole building is joined together and rises to become a holy temple in the Lord. And in You, we too are being built together to become a dwelling in which You live by Your Spirit (Eph. 2:17–22).

THE WAY WE BEHAVE OVERWHELMINGLY FLOWS FROM WHAT WE DEEPLY BELIEVE.

I am so grateful that my own heavenly Father is the Sovereign Lord who made the heavens and the earth by His great power and outstretched arm. Nothing is too hard for You! (Jer. 32:17).

Truly, You have released me to resurrection life! For through the law I died to the law so that I might live for God. I have been crucified with Christ and I no longer live, but Christ lives in me. The life I live in the body, I live by faith in the Son of God, who loved me and gave Himself for me (Gal. 2:19–20).

Lord, I belong to Christ Jesus! Therefore I have crucified the sinful nature with its passions and desires (Gal. 5:24). Help me live in the reality of this liberating crucifixion.

OBEDIENCE TO GOD IN A DIFFICULT
SITUATION WILL ULTIMATELY BEAR
FRUIT, EVEN THOUGH IT MIGHT
IMMEDIATELY CAUSE HARDSHIP.

Lord God, according to Your Word, if I wholeheartedly commit whatever I do to You, my plans will succeed (Prov. 16:3). I acknowledge that the heart of committing any plan to You is seeking *Your* plan.

Show me the right path, Father!

Please help me not to merely listen to the Word, and so deceive myself. Help me to do what it says (James 1:22). Your Word works, but if I am to experience it personally, I must be obedient. I need Your help, Lord.

When Your words come to me, help me to eat them. Make them my joy and my heart's delight, for I bear Your name, Lord God Almighty (Jer. 15:16). Increase my appetite for Your Word, my Sufficiency!

GOD'S MOTIVATION FOR SURFACING
THE DESTRUCTIVE PARTS OF US IS SO
WE WILL FACE THEM AND COOPERATE
AS HE UPROOTS AND HEALS THEM.

O Lord, have mercy on me. Heal me, for I have sinned against You (Ps. 41:4).

See how distressed I am! I am in torment within, and in my heart I am disturbed, for I have been most rebellious. Outside, the sword bereaves; inside, there is only death (Lam. 1:20). But thank You that I can be assured You will never forsake one of Your children crying out in agony over sin.

Lord God, lift me out of the slimy pit, out of the mud and mire. Set my feet on a rock and give me a firm place to stand. Put a new song in my mouth, a hymn of praise to my God! Blessed is the one who makes the Lord his trust (Ps. 40:2–4).

GOD'S MERCIES HAVE EXISTED
THROUGH ALL ETERNITY,
YET SCRIPTURE TELLS US THEY
ARE NEW EVERY MORNING.

Merciful and faithful Lord, because of Your great love I am not consumed, for Your compassions never fail. They are new every morning; great is Your faithfulness.

I say to myself, "The Lord is my portion; therefore I will wait for him." Lord, You are good to those whose hope is in You, to the one who seeks You (Lam. 3:22–25).

Surely You, Jesus, took up my infirmities and carried my sorrows, yet we considered You stricken by God, smitten by Him and afflicted. But You were pierced for my transgressions; You were crushed for my iniquities; the punishment that brought me peace was upon You, and by Your wounds, Lord Jesus, I am healed (Isa. 53:4–5).

GOD DOES NOT INSIST ON OUR FORGIVING OTHERS FOR THE SAKE OF THAT PERSON ALONE BUT FOR PEACE IN OUR OWN LIVES.

Lord, as hard as this may be for me to comprehend or rationalize, Your Word is clear: if I forgive others when they sin against me, You, my heavenly Father, will also forgive me. But if I do not forgive others their sins, You, my Father, will not forgive my sins (Matt. 6:14–15).

So empower me to bear with others and forgive whatever grievances I may have against them. Help me to forgive as You, Lord, have forgiven me (Col. 3:13).

If someone sins against me seven times in a day, and seven times comes back to me and says, "I repent," I desire to be obedient to You. Strengthen me, Lord, to forgive him, to forgive her (Luke 17:4).

GOD'S SPECIALTY IS RAISING DEAD THINGS TO LIFE AND MAKING IMPOSSIBLE THINGS POSSIBLE.

Why are you downcast, O my soul? Why so disturbed within me?

I choose to put my hope in You, O God, for I will yet praise You, my Savior and my God. My soul is downcast within me; therefore I remember You! (Ps. 42:5–6). In all my distress, You too are distressed, and the angel of Your presence saves me. In Your love and mercy You redeem me. You lift me up and carry me as You have done for Your children through all the days of old (Isa. 45:3).

Lord, help me not to fear, for You are with me; I need not be dismayed, for You are my God. You will strengthen me and help me. You will uphold me with Your righteous right hand (Isa. 41:10).

WE HAVE TO EXERCISE FAITH BEFORE
WE CAN BELIEVE WE ARE EVEN
CAPABLE OF LONG-TERM OBEDIENCE.
AND WE ARE!

Lord God, in my inner being I delight in
Your law. But I see another law at work in the
members of my body, waging war against the
law of my mind and making me a prisoner of
the law of sin at work within my members.

How wretched I am! Who will rescue me
from this body of death?

Thanks be to God—through Jesus Christ
our Lord (Rom. 7:22–25). Lord, You sent Your
Son to rescue me from this body of death! Set
me free to new life in You! I do not have to be
a prisoner to sin.

Please help me understand that the battle
which rages over my body originates in my
mind. Help me surrender my mind to You and
Your truth.

YOUR ENEMY IS STANDING ON YOUR GOD-GIVEN GROUND DARING YOU TO TAKE POSSESSION OF IT.

I will sing to You, Lord, for You are highly exalted. The horse and its rider You have hurled into the sea! You, Lord, are my strength and my song. You have become my salvation. You are my God and I will praise You.

You, Lord, are a warrior! The Lord is Your name! (Exod. 15:1–3).

Your right hand, O God, is majestic in power. Your right hand, O Lord, shatters the enemy. In the greatness of Your majesty, You will throw down those who oppose You. You will unleash Your burning anger. It will consume them like stubble (Exod. 15:6–7).

You are the Great I AM. This is Your name forever! (Exod. 3:14–15). My enemy cannot begin to stand against You.

GOD ALONE KNOWS THE ULTIMATE OBJECTIVE TO WHICH HE ALIGNS EVERY DIVINE ACT ON BEHALF OF HIS CHILDREN.

Father, it is unthinkable that You would do wrong. How I thank You that the Almighty would never pervert justice.

Who appointed you over the earth? Who put You in charge of the whole world? If it were Your intention and You withdrew Your Spirit and breath, all mankind would perish together and man would return to the dust (Job 34:12–15).

Instead, my Lord, You have promised that Your plans for Your people are plans to prosper and not to harm, plans to give us hope and a future (Jer, 29:11).

Who is like You, Lord—the One who sits enthroned on high yet stoops down to look on the heavens and the earth? (Ps. 113:5–6).

FAITH ALWAYS PLEASES GOD, EVEN IF
IT PROMPTS AN OFF-TARGET PETITION.
WE ALL ERR IN MANY WAYS. LET US
ERR ON THE SIDE OF FAITH.

Father God, according to Your Word, without faith it is impossible to please You, because anyone who comes to You must believe that You exist and that You reward those who earnestly seek You (Heb. 11:6).

Lord, I want to please You. Build faith in me so my life will honor the life of Your Son at all times, in every way.

Help me not be like the ancient Israelites who willfully put You to the test (Ps. 78:18). They did not believe in You or trust in Your deliverance even after all the wonders You had shown them (Ps. 78:22).

Please swell my soul with belief, and help me to trust emphatically in Your deliverance.

BY DEMANDING THAT WE SEEK HIS GLORY ALONE, GOD IS CALLING US TO OVERCOME THE NATURAL TEMPTATION TO SEEK OUR OWN.

Father, Your Word asks the questions, "Who is it you have insulted and blasphemed? Against whom have you raised your voice and lifted your eyes in pride? Against the Holy One of Israel!" (2 Kings 19:22).

Please help me to have a proper respect for You, O God.

A day is certainly coming, Father, when the arrogance of man will be brought low and the pride of men humbled. You alone will be exalted in that day (Isa. 2:17).

Help me to humble myself under Your mighty hand, Lord, that You may lift me up in due time (1 Pet. 5:6). Help me to humble myself now so You are free to do wonders later!

WE TEND TO RUN TO GOD FOR TEMPORARY RELIEF. GOD IS LOOKING FOR PEOPLE WHO WILL WALK WITH HIM IN STEADFAST BELIEF.

At this moment, Father, I am choosing the way of truth. I want to set my heart on Your laws (Ps. 119:30). I want to choose the way of truth the rest of my days.

Test me, O Lord, and try me. Examine my heart and my mind, for Your love is ever before me, and I desire to walk continually in Your truth (Ps. 26:2–3). Redeem me, O Lord, the God of truth (Ps. 31:5). Help me remember that nothing and no one can be redeemed without truth: the God of truth!

Show me Your ways, O Lord. Teach me Your paths. Guide me in Your truth and teach me, for You are God my Savior, and my hope is in You all day long (Ps. 25:4–5).

THE PURE-HEARTED, FAITH-FILLED
PETITIONER IS GOING TO BEHOLD A
MIRACLE, WHETHER TEMPORAL OR
ETERNAL. WONDERS NEVER CEASE.

I give thanks to You, Lord, for You are good. Your love endures forever.

I give thanks to You, the God of gods. I give thanks to You, the Lord of lords, to You who alone does great wonders, who by Your understanding made the heavens, who spread out the earth upon the waters, who made the great lights and the sun to govern the day.

Your love endures forever.

I give thanks to You, Lord, the One who remembered me in my low estate and freed me from my enemies.

I give thanks to the God of heaven, for Your love endures forever. Indeed, Your love endures forever! (Ps. 136:1–8, 23–26).

IF OUR MINDS WOULD ABSORB THAT WE ARE ACCEPTED BY GOD IN CHRIST, OUR CHOICES AND BEHAVIORS WOULD BE PROFOUNDLY AFFECTED.

Lord, I am so grateful to be one of Your chosen people, part of a royal priesthood, a holy nation, a people belonging to You, God, that I may declare the praises of You who called me out of darkness into Your wonderful light (1 Pet. 2:9).

You pose the question in Your Word, "Can a mother forget the baby at her breast and have no compassion on the child she has borne?" You assure me that though she may forget, You will absolutely never forget me! You have engraved me on the palms of Your hands (Isa. 49:15–16).

For the sake of Your great name, You will not reject Your people. You have been pleased to make me Your own (1 Sam. 12:22).

God creates and activates a nagging dissatisfaction in us for an excellent reason—He wants us to come to repentance.

Father, Your Word promises me that the one who conceals his sins does not prosper, but whoever confesses and renounces them finds mercy (Prov. 28:13). Your Word also says that if we claim to be without sin, we deceive ourselves, and the truth is not in us (1 John 1:8).

Help me, Lord! I need Your truth in me! Lord, I confess all my sins to You right now—specifically—by name—and I thank You that You are always faithful and just to forgive me of all my sin and purify me from all unrighteousness (1 John 1:9). As a believer in Your Son, Jesus Christ, I am under grace, not under law (Rom. 6:14). Therefore, sin does not have permission to be my master.

GOD CARES MORE FOR OUR FREEDOM
THAN EVEN WE DO. HE INITIATED THE
SAVING RELATIONSHIP BETWEEN HIS
PEOPLE AND THEIR LIBERATOR.

O Lord, like David, help me rejoice in Your strength and say of You, "How great is my joy in the victories You give!" Father, please grant me the desire of my heart to be free from the strongholds in my life. Do not withhold the request of my lips (Ps. 21:1–2).

For I know that my old self was crucified with You, so that this body of sin might be done away with, that I should no longer be a slave to sin—because anyone who has died has been freed from sin (Rom. 6:6–7).

I acknowledge that it is for freedom that Christ has set me free. Your desire is for me to stand firm and not let myself be burdened again by the yoke of slavery (Gal. 5:1).

Help me, Lord. Empower me!

OUR GOD OF GRACE FORGIVES THE AUTHENTICALLY REPENTANT AND "NO, NEVER" COUNTS THEIR SINS AGAINST THEM.

Lord God, I count on You not to withhold Your mercy from me. May Your love and Your truth always protect me. For troubles without number surround me. My sins have overtaken me, and I cannot see. They are more than the hairs of my head, and my heart fails within me (Ps. 40:11–12).

But Father, I thank You that if my heart has been responsive and I have humbled myself before You, and if I have had a heart like those who tore their robes and wept in Your presence, then I can know You have heard me, Lord (2 Kings 22:19).

I acknowledged my sin to You. I did not cover up my iniquity. And You have forgiven the guilt of my sin (Ps. 32:5).

Sometimes god may prioritize performing a miracle on our hearts and minds over a miracle concerning our circumstances.

Though the fig tree does not bud and there are no grapes on the vines, though the olive crop fails and the fields produce no food, though there are no sheep in the pen and no cattle in the stalls, yet I will rejoice in You, my Lord. I will be joyful in God, my Savior.

For You, Lord, are my strength. You make my feet like the feet of a deer. You enable me to go on the heights (Hab. 3:17–19). How inconceivable but true that You can take me to heights far exceeding the depths I have known.

Father, continue to bring me along so that I can rejoice in my sufferings, because I know suffering produces perseverance (Rom. 5:3).

GOD'S NEW TESTAMENT MATH SPECIALIZES IN ADDITION AND MULTIPLICATION, NOT SUBTRACTION AND DIVISION.

I know, Father, according to Your Word, that if I judge others, I too will be judged. With the same measure I use, it will be measured to me (Matt. 7:1–2).

When I want so badly to judge or condemn or refuse forgiveness to another, I can hear Your Word speak to my heart, saying, "If you are without sin, be the first to throw a stone at them" (John 8:7).

Help me to speak and act as those who are going to be judged by the law that gives freedom, because judgment without mercy will be shown to anyone who has not been merciful toward others. Mercy triumphs over judgment! (James 2:12–13).

God is intimately acquainted with sorrow and suffering. He also has a remedy. He is the meeter of our needs.

Lord, I don't want to be like those on the road to Emmaus, who stood still with their faces downcast when You asked, "What are you discussing together as you walk along?" They responded, "We had hoped that he was the one who was going to redeem Israel" (Luke 24:17, 21).

They did not understand that the cross had to come before the kingdom. How foolish they were! The very death which they had responded to with hopelessness represented the greatest hope of all time!

Lord God, I ask forgiveness for every single time I have blamed my hopelessness on You. You are the God of hope. You are the Blessed Hope Himself.

Sometimes the hardest biblical truths for us to accept are the ones about us.

You, God, created my inmost being. You knit me together in my mother's womb. I praise You because I am fearfully and wonderfully made. Your works are wonderful. I know that full well (Ps. 139:13–14).

Father, my body is not horrible. I know that. I have simply misused it. Please sanctify it and take it over completely.

I know, Lord, that my body is a temple of the Holy Spirit who is in me, whom I have received from You. I am not my own; I was bought at a price. Therefore I desire to honor You with my body (1 Cor. 6:19–20).

WE LEARN TO BE VICTORIOUS
BY SURRENDERING OUR LIVES
TO GOD, NOT BY GRITTING OUR
TEETH AND TRYING HARDER.

Lord God, the enemy boasted, "I will pursue, I will overtake them. I will divide the spoils; I will gorge myself on them. I will draw my sword, and my hand will destroy them."

But You can blow with Your breath and cause the sea to cover my enemy! You, Lord, can cause my enemy to sink like lead in the mighty waters! (Exod. 15:9–10).

Lord, Your power has not diminished since the days when You revealed Your power and glory as You fought for Israel. I am Your child, too. Fight for me, God! Overpower the one who seeks to overpower me!

FEBRUARY

IF WE CAN COME UP WITH A GOD WE CAN FULLY EXPLAIN, WE HAVE COME UP WITH A DIFFERENT GOD THAN THE BIBLE'S.

Yours, my Lord, is the greatness and the power and the glory and the majesty and the splendor, for everything in heaven and earth is Yours.

Yours, my own heavenly Father, is the kingdom, and You are exalted as head above all (1 Chron. 29:11).

Lord, I know that You are great—greater than all gods. You do whatever pleases You in the heavens and on the earth, in the seas and all their depths (Ps. 135:5).

Yet although You are sovereign and do what You please, You are righteous in all Your ways. You are loving toward all You have made (Ps. 145:7).

THE CHAINS BEGIN TO BREAK WHEN WE ARE WILLING TO BELIEVE WE ARE WHO GOD SAYS WE ARE.

Father God, Your Word declares that we, Your people, are Your witnesses and Your servants whom You have chosen, that we may know and believe You and understand that You are God. Before You no god was formed, nor will there be one after You (Isa. 43:10).

You have chosen me, God, for the express purpose of knowing and believing You. But I can't really begin to know You until I choose to believe You!

According to Your Word, it is possible to be broken off from part of Your plan because of unbelief. Your Word says not to be arrogant but to be afraid (Rom. 11:20). I do not want to miss any part of Your plan because of my own unbelief! Help me walk by faith.

YOU DO HAVE A CHOICE. YOU DON'T
HAVE TO DO IT GOD'S WAY. BUT I'LL
PROMISE YOU THIS: THERE IS NO HIGH
LIKE THE MOST HIGH.

Lord, according to Your Word, after King Uzziah became powerful, his pride led to his downfall. He was unfaithful to the Lord his God (2 Chron. 26:16).

Your Word also tells of the time that King Hezekiah repented of the pride of his heart, as did the people of Jerusalem. Therefore, the Lord's wrath did not come upon them during the days of Hezekiah (2 Chron. 32:26).

Please help me, Lord, not to allow pride to be my downfall. Thank You for forgiving me when I repent of the pride of my heart.

Truly, Your eyes are on the haughty to bring them low, but You, my Lord and my God, save the humble (2 Sam. 22:28).

WE CAN BE MISERABLY DISSATISFIED IF WE ACCEPT CHRIST'S SALVATION YET REJECT THE FULLNESS OF DAILY RELATIONSHIP THAT SATISFIES.

Do not withhold Your mercy from me, O Lord. May Your love and Your truth always protect me (Ps. 40:11). Help me to learn how much Your truth protects me, Father. Without it, I am vulnerable to the enemy and to my own flesh nature.

O God, send forth Your light and Your truth into my life. Let them guide me; let them bring me to Your holy mountain, to the place where You dwell (Ps. 43:3).

Surely You desire truth in my inner parts. You teach me wisdom in the inmost place (Ps. 51:6). Please expose to me the deeply embedded lies I've believed, Lord, and replace them with permanently engraved truth.

PRAYERLESSNESS IS THE MOST PROHIBITIVE OBSTACLE IN THE ROAD TO A BELIEVER'S VICTORY, NO MATTER WHAT OUR SPECIFIC PURSUIT MAY BE.

I call on You, O God, for You will answer me. Give ear to me and hear my prayer. Show the wonder of Your great love, You who save by Your right hand those who take refuge in You from their foes. Keep me as the apple of Your eye. Hide me in the shadow of Your wings (Ps. 17:6–8).

Show me Your ways, O Lord. Teach me Your paths. Guide me in Your truth and teach me, for You are God my Savior, and my hope is in You all day long.

Remember Your great mercy and love, for they are from of old. Remember not the sins of my youth and my rebellious ways. Instead, remember me according to Your love, for You are good, O Lord (Ps. 25:4–7).

AS LONG AS THE SUN COMES UP IN THE MORNING, GOD WILL KEEP OFFERING TO DELIVER HIS CHILDREN.

Lord God, just as Your children the Israelites were chosen out of all the peoples on the face of the earth to be Your people, Your treasured possession, I believe that we, the body of Christ, have been too.

You did not set Your affection on Your children and choose us because we were more numerous than other peoples. It was because You loved us that You redeemed us from slavery and from the power of the enemy.

Help me to know with certainty that You, the Lord my God, are indeed God—the faithful God, keeping Your covenant of love to a thousand generations of those who love You and keep Your commands (Deut. 7:6–9).

REFUSE TO LET YOUR ENEMY PLUCK
AWAY THE SEEDS GOD HAS PLANTED.
LET THESE TRUTHS TAKE ROOT, AND
CULTIVATE THEM WITH BELIEF.

Oh Lord, You have searched me and You know me. You know when I sit and when I rise. You perceive my thoughts from afar. You discern my going out and my lying down. You are familiar with all my ways. Before a word is on my tongue, You know it completely.

You hem me in—behind and before. You have laid Your hand upon me. I do not need to feel shame or fear in Your intimate knowledge of every detail of my life, because Your Word says that Your knowledge of me is wonderful! (Ps. 139:1–6). Thank You, Father.

So please forgive my self-loathing. Help me to praise You because I am fearfully and wonderfully made. Your works are wonderful. I know that full well (Ps. 139:14).

WE FEAR MAKING SACRIFICES. BUT THE IRONY IS THAT WE MAKE A LOT OF SACRIFICES WHEN WE ARE NOT LIVING THE WILL OF GOD.

Father, the false teachers of this world promise freedom, while they themselves are slaves of depravity—for a man is a slave to whatever has mastered him (2 Pet. 2:19).

Lord, I acknowledge my slavery to certain sins, and I deeply desire to be mastered by You alone. Only Your mastery brings liberty.

"Everything is permissible for me"—but not everything is beneficial. "Everything is permissible for me"—but I desire not to be mastered by anything (1 Cor. 6:12).

Lord God, help me to recognize and discern what is not beneficial for me. Help me to see that authentic liberty is being free to do certain things and free not to do others.

GOD DOES NOT CONDEMN YOU. HE CALLS YOU. WILL YOU OPEN YOUR HAND TO HIM AND LET GO OF YOUR IDOLS? HE IS OPENING HIS TO YOU.

Father, I praise You with my whole heart that when the wicked forsakes his ways and the evil man his thoughts—when he turns to You—You will have mercy on him, for You will freely pardon! (Isa. 55:7).

How thankful I am that You have had mercy on me according to Your unfailing love. According to Your great compassion, You blot out my transgressions. You can wash away all my iniquity and cleanse me from my sin.

You can create in me a pure heart, O God, and renew a steadfast spirit within me (Ps. 51:1–2, 10).

Lord, You have heard me cry for mercy. You accept my prayer (Ps. 6:9).

OUR CALLINGS COULD BE AT STAKE IF WE DON'T ALLOW GOD TO DEAL WITH OUR CHRONIC INSECURITIES.

Lord, I don't want to waver through unbelief regarding Your promises, but I desire to be strengthened in my faith and give glory to You, being fully persuaded that You have the power to do what You promise. You credit this kind of faith to Your children as righteousness! (Rom. 4:20–22).

As a bridegroom rejoices over his bride, so will You rejoice over me (Isa. 64:5b).

Even to my old age and gray hair, You are the One who will sustain me. You made me and You will carry me; You will sustain and You will rescue me. I will remember the former things, those of long ago. You are God, and there is no other! You are God, and there is none like You! (Isa. 46:4, 9).

CONCENTRATING ON THE SHORTCOMINGS OF OTHERS CAN CHEAT A CHRISTIAN OF TRULY ENJOYING THE PRESENCE OF GOD.

Lord, I must ask myself why I look at the speck of sawdust in another person's eye and pay no attention to the plank in my own eye.

How can I say to my brother, "Let me take the speck out of your eye," when all the time there is a plank in my own eye?

O God, rescue me from being a hypocrite! Give me the honesty and courage to first take the plank out of my own eye, and then I may see clearly to remove the speck from another person's eye (Matt. 7:3–5).

I am not without sin. If I claim to be without sin, I deceive myself, and the truth is not in me (1 John 1:8).

WE MUST NEVER CEASE BELIEVING THAT GOD CARES ABOUT THOSE IN PHYSICAL, EMOTIONAL, MENTAL, OR SPIRITUAL PRISONS.

Jesus, the Lord has anointed You to preach good news to the poor. He has sent You to bind up the brokenhearted, to proclaim freedom for the captives and release from darkness for the prisoners, to proclaim the year of the Lord's favor and the day of vengeance of our God.

You comfort all who mourn. You provide for those who grieve in Zion—to bestow on us a crown of beauty instead of ashes, the oil of gladness instead of mourning, and a garment of praise instead of a spirit of despair (Isa. 61:1–3a).

I am hard pressed on every side, but I don't have to be crushed. I am perplexed, but I do not have to be in despair (2 Cor. 4:8).

WE MUST BEGIN TO REMOVE IDOLS BY CHOOSING TO RECOGNIZE THEIR EXISTENCE AND ADMITTING THEIR INABILITY TO KEEP US SATISFIED.

Lord God, according to Your Word, no one who is born of God will continue to sin, because God's seed remains in him (1 John 3:9). Please help me understand that I cannot simply go on and on indefinitely in my sin and claim to belong to You.

O God, if Your Spirit does not presently dwell in me, and if I'm not saved from an eternal destiny in hell, please open my eyes and bring me to Your salvation!

This then is how I know that I belong to the truth. This is how I set my heart at rest in Your presence whenever my heart condemns me. For You, God, are greater than my heart, and You know everything (1 John 3:19).

TO LIVE IN THE FREEDOM GOD HAS PURPOSED FOR US, WE MUST RECOGNIZE AND FORSAKE ALL OTHER GODS.

Lord God, when Your children, the Israelites, were defeated in battle, You revealed to them that they were hanging on to something that did not belong to them. You said, "You cannot stand against your enemies until you remove it" (Josh. 7:13).

Father God, I earnestly ask You to reveal anything in my life that could be hindering victory, then give me the courage to release it to You.

Keep me safe, O God, for in You and You alone I take refuge. I say to You, Lord, "You are my Lord; Apart from you I have no good thing" (Ps. 16:1–2).

OUR PART IS TO BELIEVE GOD. HIS PART IS TO BE GOD AND DO WHAT IS ULTIMATELY AND ETERNALLY BEST.

God, You made the world and everything in it. You are the Lord of heaven and earth, and You do not live in temples built by hands, as if You needed anything, because You Yourself give all men life and breath and everything else.

From one man You made every nation of men, that they should inhabit the whole earth. And You determined the times set for them and the exact places where they should live. You did this so that men would seek You and perhaps reach out for You and find You, though You are not far from each one of us.

For in You we live and move and have our being (Acts 17:24–28).

GOD MOST OFTEN LOOKS FOR WHAT PREVAILS IN OUR LIVES. IF UNBELIEF PREVAILS, WE WILL FIND OURSELVES REPEATING OUR CYCLES OF DEFEAT.

Merciful Father, Your Word says that if people do not persist in unbelief, they can be grafted back into the fullness of Your plan (Rom. 11:23). Thank You, God, for so often granting the gift of second chances!

I don't want to be like the ancient Israelites who were not able to enter the Promised Land because of their unbelief (Heb. 3:19). In spite of Your chastisement, they kept on sinning. In spite of Your wonders, they did not believe, so You ended their days in futility (Ps. 78:32–33).

O Lord, I don't want my days to end in futility. I want to be able to participate fully in what You're doing in my generation.

WE MAY BE AFRAID TO ASK GOD TO
KEEP US HUMBLE. WHY ARE WE NOT
FAR MORE FRIGHTENED OF WHAT
PRIDE CAN DO?

Father, according to Your Word, in his pride the wicked person does not seek You. In all his thoughts, there is no room for You (Ps. 10:4). Please help me to always make room in my thoughts for You, God. Don't allow me to continue on in pride and stop seeking You.

Your Word clearly warns us that pride goes before destruction, a haughty spirit before a fall (Prov. 16:18).

God, I know that a man's pride brings him low, but a man of lowly spirit gains honor (Prov. 29:23). Help me to understand what You mean by a lowly and humble spirit. I want to be a person who gains honor in Your sight, O Lord.

GOD IS NOT LOOKING FOR
SPIRITUAL GIANTS. HE IS LOOKING
FOR BELIEVERS WHO BELIEVE
FOR A CHANGE.

Teach me Your way, O Lord, and I will walk in Your truth. Give me an undivided heart, that I may fear Your name (Ps. 86:11). Do not allow anything to snatch the word of truth from my mouth, Lord, for I have put my hope in Your laws (Ps. 119:43).

Glorious God, in Your majesty ride forth victoriously in behalf of truth, humility, and righteousness. Let Your right hand display awesome deeds (Ps. 45:4). I don't need to be afraid of truth. It is the key You will use to take me forth to victory.

You are near to all who call on You, Lord, to all who call on You in truth (Ps. 145:18).

WHEN WE ALLOW THE PRINCE OF PEACE TO GOVERN OUR LIVES, PEACE EITHER IMMEDIATELY OR ULTIMATELY RESULTS.

O God, though the mountains be shaken and the hills be removed, yet Your unfailing love for me will not be shaken, nor Your covenant of peace be removed. You are the Lord who has compassion on me (Isa. 54:10). Thank You, God.

Like Jonah, help me to be convinced that You are slow to anger and abounding in love (Jon. 4:2). But unlike Jonah, help me to delight in Your compassionate ways, O God, for I am such a recipient of Your grace and mercy.

Jesus Christ, my Kinsman Redeemer and my Bridegroom, Your banner over me is love! (Song of Sol. 2:4).

THE GLORY OF GOD ALWAYS HAS AN
IMPACT. WHEN HIS GLORY APPEARS,
IT JUST CAN'T HELP BUT INTERRUPT
ANY ROUTINE.

I thank You, my God, who always leads me in triumphal procession in Christ and through me desires to spread everywhere the fragrance of the knowledge of Him. For You have called me to be the aroma of Christ among those who are being saved as well as those who are perishing (2 Cor. 2:14–15).

Father God, I ask You to lead me when I'm blinded by ways I have not known. Along unfamiliar paths, please guide me.

Turn the darkness into light before me, Lord, and make the rough places smooth. I pray these are the things You will do, for I know You will not forsake me (Isa. 42:16).

SOME BELIEVERS HAVE THE MATURITY TO HELP FREE US FROM OUR GRAVE CLOTHES, AND OTHERS JUST KEEP HANDING THEM BACK.

Father, Your Word says that he who walks with the wise grows wise, but a companion of fools suffers harm (Prov. 13:20).

Your Word also says that fools mock at making amends for sin, but goodwill is found among the upright (Prov. 14:9). Help me to make any necessary amends for hurts I may have caused.

Help me also to forgive and release anyone who had to confront or wound my heart in an effort to help me find wholeness. Your Word says that open rebuke is better than hidden love, and that wounds from a friend can be trusted, but an enemy multiplies kisses (Prov. 27:5–6). Thank You, Lord, for giving me the right kind of companions.

A CHRISTIAN IS HELD CAPTIVE BY ANYTHING THAT HINDERS THE ABUNDANT, EFFECTIVE, SPIRIT-FILLED LIFE GOD PLANNED FOR HIM.

God, according to Your liberating Word, I was called to be free. But help me not to use my freedom to indulge the sinful nature. Rather, strengthen me to serve others in love (Gal. 5:13).

Help my soul to find rest in You alone. My hope comes from You. You alone are my rock and my salvation. You are my fortress; I will not be shaken.

My salvation and honor depend on You, God. You are my mighty rock, my refuge.

Help me, Lord, to trust in You at all times. Remind me to pour out my heart to You, for You, God, are my refuge (Ps. 62:5–8).

OBEDIENT LIVES ARE NOT PERFECT LIVES. OBEDIENCE DOES NOT MEAN SINLESSNESS BUT CONFESSION AND REPENTANCE WHEN WE SIN.

Sorrow has led me to repentance. I pray that I have been sorrowful as You intended, that I was helped rather than hurt by the confrontation of my sin. Thank You for the godly sorrow that brings repentance leading to salvation and leaving no regret (2 Cor. 7:9–10).

Father, You promised that those who sow in tears will reap with songs of joy. Those who go out weeping, carrying seed to sow, will return with songs of joy, carrying sheaves with them (Ps. 126:5–6).

Lord, I have come with weeping. I have prayed as You brought me back. You will lead me beside streams of water on a level path where I will not stumble, because You are my Father (Jer. 31:9).

SUFFERING IS A COMPULSORY PART OF HUMAN EXISTENCE. THE DIFFERENCE FOR BELIEVERS IS THAT SUFFERING NEED NEVER BE IN VAIN.

Lord, as I consider what You do, I find myself feeling at times like the writer of Ecclesiastes: Who can straighten what You have made crooked? When times are good, I am to be happy. But when times are bad, consider: You have made the one as well as the other (Eccles. 7:13–14).

According to Your Word, Lord, there is a time for everything, and a season for every activity under heaven: a time to be born and a time to die, a time to plant and a time to uproot, a time to weep and a time to laugh, a time to mourn and a time to dance (Eccles. 3:1–2, 4).

Truly, You are the Creator and Sustainer of time. Nothing is "untimely" to You.

GOD WANTS TO TRANSFORM AND RENEW OUR MINDS SO WE CAN THINK THE THOUGHTS OF CHRIST ABOUT THE PERSON WE ARE TO FORGIVE.

Jesus, when Peter asked You, "Lord, how many times shall I forgive my brother when he sins against me? Up to seven times?" You responded, "I tell you, not seven times, but seventy-seven times" (Matt. 18:21–22).

In the parable of the unmerciful servant, the only person in the end who was imprisoned and tortured was the one who would not forgive (Matt. 18:33–34).

Help me to see the monumental price of unforgiveness. It is so enslaving and torturous. According to Matthew 18:35, You may allow me to suffer the same kind of repercussions if I refuse to forgive from my heart someone who has sinned against me.

WILL WE LET SATAN CLEAN OUR CARCASSES TO THE BONE BECAUSE WE LET THEM DROP IN A DESERT OF DEFEAT?

Lord God, I cry out to You. My spirit grows faint within me. My heart within me is dismayed (Ps. 143:4). Answer me when I call to You, O my righteous God. Give me relief from my distress. Be merciful to me and hear my prayer (Ps. 4:1).

In my distress I call to You, Lord. I cry to my God for help. And from Your temple You hear my voice. My cry comes before You, into Your ears (Ps. 18:6).

My soul is downcast within me, yet this I call to mind and therefore I have hope: Because of Your great love I am not consumed, for Your compassions never fail. They are new every morning. Great, O Lord, is Your faithfulness! (Lam. 3:21–23).

HOW MANY TIMES HAVE I FED ON ASHES INSTEAD OF FEASTING ON THE WORD? HOW MANY TIMES HAS MY DELUDED HEART MISLED ME?

Lord, I do not understand what I do. For what I want to do, I do not do, but what I hate, I do. Sin is living in me.

I know that nothing good lives in me—that is, in my sinful nature. For I have the desire to do what is good, but I cannot carry it out. For what I do is not the good I want to do. No, the evil I do not want to do—this I keep on doing. So I find this law at work: when I want to do good, evil is right there with me (Rom. 7:15–21).

Lord, I have come to understand that my heart is deceitful above all things (Jer. 17:9). Please help me recognize the ways my heart and my feelings are deceiving me.

IF WE KEEP FIGHTING OUR OWN INNER BATTLES. WE'LL NEVER HAVE THE STRENGTH TO STAND UP AND FIGHT OUR TRUE ENEMY.

O God, how I thank You for seeing my misery and hearing my cries because of Satan, the slave driver. You are concerned about my suffering. Come down to rescue me, O Lord, and bring me to Your place of promise (Exod. 3:7–8).

Who among the gods is like You, Lord— majestic in holiness, awesome in glory, working wonders? Stretch out Your right hand and deal with my enemy, God! (Exod. 15:11–12).

I thank You that those who belong to You were meant to be the head, not the tail! If I am obedient to You and do not turn aside from Your ways, You will not allow the enemy to keep me at the bottom (Deut. 28:13–14).

EVERY DAY THE SUN RISES BY GOD'S
PERMISSION. HE'S NEVER HAD A WINK
OF SLEEP. HE'S BEEN GOD THROUGH
EVERY DAY OF YOUR HERITAGE.

My Father, Your kingdom is an everlasting kingdom, and Your dominion endures throughout all generations. You, my Lord, are faithful to all Your promises and loving toward all You have made (Ps. 145:13).

Many, O Lord my God, are the wonders You have done. The things You planned for us, no one can recount to You. Were I to speak of them, they would be too many for me to declare (Ps. 40:5).

Lord, You have been our dwelling place throughout all generations. Before the mountains were born, before You brought forth the earth and the world, from everlasting to everlasting, You are God (Ps. 90:1–2).

MARCH

WHETHER OR NOT WE LIKE THE CONCEPT, CHRIST LOVES TO RESPOND TO US ACCORDING TO OUR FAITH.

Lord Jesus, before You healed the blind men who cried out for Your mercy, You asked them, "Do you believe that I am able to do this?"

After they replied to You by saying, "Yes, Lord," You touched their eyes and You said, "According to your faith will it be done to you" (Matt. 9:28–29).

Clearly, my faith impacts what You are willing to perform in my life. Please help me to believe that You are able.

Lord, I want to be like the one to whom You said, "Woman, you have great faith! Your request is granted" (Matt. 15:28). Flourish this kind of faith in me, God!

THE MOST EFFECTIVE MEANS THE ENEMY HAS TO KEEP BELIEVERS FROM BEING FULL OF THE SPIRIT IS TO KEEP US FULL OF OURSELVES.

Lord, Your Word speaks of the wicked wearing pride as their necklace, and clothing themselves with violence (Ps. 73:6). You indicate a link between pride and violence. Please cause my life to be void of both these evils.

You're teaching me that pride only breeds quarrels, but wisdom is found in those that take advice (Prov. 13:10). Help me to discern the pride that is involved when I am quarrelsome.

Father, You've said that to fear the Lord is to hate evil. You hate pride and arrogance, evil behavior, and perverse speech (Prov. 8:13). Help me to have a healthy fear of You that abolishes pride and arrogance.

Like the son was with the father, we must be committed to god's right to rule, and convinced that god's rule is right.

Father, Your Word exhorts us to buy the truth and never sell it—to get wisdom, discipline, and understanding (Prov. 23:23). Help me understand that sometimes truth is costly but not nearly as costly as deception. Truth will never fail to return enormous dividends.

If I'm really going to be one of Your disciples, I must hold to Your teaching. Then I will know the truth, and the truth will set me free (John 8:31–32). Help me to see the vital link between Your truth and my liberty.

Father God, continue to teach me. Help me to recognize what is in accordance with the truth that is in Jesus (Eph. 4:21).

PLACE YOUR EAR AGAINST THE CHEST OF THE SAVIOR, AND HEAR THE STEADY PULSE OF THE BOUNDLESS LOVE THAT HOLDS YOU.

How I thank You, God, that You heal my waywardness. You love me freely (Hos. 14:4). Help me not only to fully accept how much You love me, but help me to abide in Your love (John 15:9, NASB).

I am unspeakably grateful that You have demonstrated Your own love for me in this: while I was still a sinner, Christ died for me (Rom. 5:8).

You, God, loved me so much that You have given Your one and only Son. And since I believe in Him, I shall not perish but have eternal life. For You did not send Your Son into the world to condemn me but to save me through Him (John 3:16–17).

SUFFERING HAS AN UNDENIABLE ROLE IN THE NEW TESTAMENT AND UNDER THE NEW COVENANT.

Lord God, according to Your Word, Your Spirit Himself testifies with our spirit that we are Your children. Now if we are children, then we are heirs—heirs of Yours and coheirs with Christ, if indeed we share in His sufferings in order that we may also share in His glory.

Help me to really embrace the truth that any present sufferings I encounter are not worth comparing with the glory that will be revealed in me (Rom. 8:16–18).

Lord Jesus, just as Your sufferings flow over into our lives, so also through You our comfort overflows (2 Cor. 1:5). You are so faithful, Jesus.

THE FREEDOM OF CHRIST IS WORTH THE SURRENDER OF ABSOLUTELY ANYTHING. RELIEF, NOT REMORSE, AWAITS THE REPENTANT.

Father, Your Word says that a person who lacks self-control is like a city whose walls are broken down (Prov. 25:28).

Sometimes I feel like there is so much rubble, I can't rebuild the wall (Neh. 4:10). But Your Word claims that You are the Repairer of Broken Walls, and the Restorer of Streets with Dwellings (Isa. 58:12). Please introduce Yourself to me by these wonderful names and rebuild the rubble in my life.

I confess to You that I am overwhelmed by the task ahead, but I am thankful that You have authority over all things. Heaven is Your throne; earth is Your footstool (Matt. 5:35). Therefore, anything over my head is under Your feet!

SATAN'S SPECIALTY IS PSYCHOLOGICAL WARFARE. IF HE CAN TURN US ON GOD, OTHERS, OR OURSELVES, WE WON'T TURN ON HIM.

In view of Your mercy, Lord, I offer my body as a living sacrifice, holy and pleasing to You. This is my spiritual act of worship.

I desire not to be conformed any longer to the pattern of this world, but to be transformed by the renewing of my mind. Then I will be able to test and approve what Your will is—Your good, pleasing, and perfect will (Rom. 12:1–2).

Lord, I have too long given the devil a foothold (Eph. 4:27). Please help me to stop offering him so many opportunities to bring defeat into my life. Your plan for me is victory. I can do everything through You, Lord Jesus, because You give me strength (Phil. 4:13).

TO EXPERIENCE THE KIND OF PEACE THAT COVERS ALL CIRCUMSTANCES, THE BIBLE CHALLENGES US TO ACTIVE, AUTHENTIC PRAYER LIVES.

O merciful God, when a prayer or plea is made by any of Your people—each one aware of his afflictions and pains, spreading out his hands toward You—then hear from heaven, Your dwelling place.

Forgive, and deal with each man according to all he does, since You know his heart (for You alone know the hearts of men), so that they will fear You and walk in Your ways all the time they live in the land You gave our fathers (2 Chron. 6:29–31).

I thank You for the assurance that You will not despise a broken and contrite heart. Indeed, the sacrifices of God are a broken spirit (Ps. 51:17).

CHRIST DOES NOT ALWAYS IMMEDIATELY CALM THE STORM, BUT HE IS ALWAYS WILLING TO CALM HIS CHILD ON THE BASIS OF HIS PRESENCE.

Praise be to You, the Father of compassion and the God of all comfort, who comforts me in all my troubles, so that I can comfort those in any trouble with the comfort I have received from You (2 Cor. 1:3–4). You are the only one who can turn misery into ministry.

Oh, the depth of the riches of Your wisdom and knowledge, O God! How unsearchable Your judgments, and Your paths beyond tracing out!

Who has known Your mind? Or who has been Your counselor? Who has ever given to You that You should repay him? For from You and through You and to You are all things. To You be the glory forever! (Rom. 11:33–36).

FORGIVENESS INVOLVES HANDING
OVER TO GOD THE RESPONSIBILITY
FOR JUSTICE. THE LONGER WE HOLD
ONTO IT, THE MORE IT STRANGLES US.

Lord, at whatever point I judge another person, Your Word says I am condemning myself, because those of us who pass judgment do the same things.

Now I know that Your judgment against those who do such things is based on truth. So when I, a mere human, pass judgment on others and yet do the same things, do I think I will escape Your judgment? (Rom. 2:1–2).

If I do not judge, I will not be judged. If I do not condemn, I will not be condemned. If I forgive, I will be forgiven (Luke 6:37).

Help me, Lord, to extend more grace, and I will continue to receive more grace!

THE LEVEL OF TRUST WE HAVE FOR GOD IS A MONUMENTAL ISSUE IN THE LIFE OF EVERY BELIEVER.

God, even in this difficult place, You have treasures for me here. You will give me the treasures of darkness, riches stored in secret places, so that I may know that You are the Lord, the God of Israel, who summons me by name (Isa. 45:3). You want me to discover the riches of relationship with You that will set me free from this place.

You have not run away from being my Shepherd. I know You have not desired the day of despair. What passes my lips is open before You (Jer. 17:16).

Therefore, hope does not disappoint me, Lord, because You have poured out Your love into my heart by the Holy Spirit whom You have given me (Rom. 5:5).

HUMILITY TAKES A SUPPLY OF SUPERNATURAL STRENGTH THAT COMES ONLY TO THOSE STRONG ENOUGH TO ADMIT WEAKNESS.

Lord Jesus, I acknowledge to You that I have been led astray. But I know the reason You appeared on this earth, Lord, was to die for us and be raised again to destroy the devil's work (I John 3:7–8).

Lord, I have been a willing party to the devil's work. Please destroy the works he has accomplished in me and through me. Set me apart for Your work henceforth, O God.

I willingly admit I am weak in my natural self. I used to offer the parts of my body in slavery to impurity, giving in to ever-increasing wickedness. But I now offer them in slavery to righteousness leading to holiness (Rom. 6:19).

SATAN WILL TRY TO STIR UP WHAT
THE REFINER WANTS TO SKIM OFF.
HE WILL TRY TO USE OUR BINDING
ROPES TO TIE US IN KNOTS.

There is no one like You, God, who rides
on the heavens to help me, and who rides on
the clouds in Your majesty! You, the eternal
God, are my refuge. And underneath me are
Your everlasting arms. You will drive out my
enemy before me, saying, "Destroy him!"
(Deut. 33:26–27).

Who is like Your children, O God, a people saved by the Lord? You are my shield and
helper and my glorious sword. Cause my enemy
to cower, Lord! Trample down his high places
(Deut. 33:29).

My whole being exclaims, "Who is like
You, O Lord? You rescue the poor from those
too strong for them, the poor and needy from
those who rob them" (Ps. 35:10).

GOD'S GLORY FAR EXCEEDS ANYTHING
WE CAN COMPREHEND. HIS GLORY IS
EVERYTHING WE KNOW ABOUT HIM
AND INFINITELY MORE.

How great You are, my God! You are beyond my understanding! The number of Your years is past finding out.

You draw up the drops of water, which distill as rain to the streams. The clouds pour down their moisture, and abundant showers fall on mankind. Who can understand how You spread out the clouds, how You thunder from Your pavilion? (Job 36:26–29).

You are the One who forms the mountain, creates the wind, and reveals His thoughts to man. You are the One who turns dawn to darkness, and who treads the high places of the earth—the Lord God Almighty is Your name! (Amos 4:13).

THE KEY TO ANSWERED PRAYER IS
SHARING THE MIND OF CHRIST OVER
ANY GIVEN MATTER THROUGH HIS
WORDS ACTIVELY ABIDING IN US.

Father, Your Word says that if Your disciples believe, they will receive whatever they ask for in prayer (Matt. 21:22). Lord, as You mature me in my faith, teach me how to pray and what to ask of You in prayer. I have so much to learn. Keep teaching me, Father.

Lord Jesus, according to Your Word, You are not bothered by our requests. Once, when others told a synagogue ruler not to bother You any more with his request, You ignored what they said and told the man, "Don't be afraid; just believe" (Mark 5:35–36).

Help me not to be discouraged when I pray. Help me not to be afraid—but believe!

Any "no" an earnestly seeking child of God receives from the throne is for the sake of a greater "yes."

Father, help me to remember in my impatience that the end of a matter is better than its beginning, and patience is better than pride (Eccles. 7:8).

You led Your children, the Israelites, all the way in the desert for forty years, to humble them and to test them in order to know what was in their hearts, whether or not they would keep Your commands (Deut. 8:2).

Help me to understand that sometimes You lead me on certain paths to humble me also, to see what is in my heart.

Purify my heart, Lord, so that I will be patient in the waiting times, and so that You will take joy in what You find.

STAYING CLOSE TO GOD THROUGH
CONSTANT COMMUNICATION, WE
RECEIVE A CONTINUAL SUPPLY OF
STRENGTH TO WALK VICTORIOUSLY.

Father, You tell us in Your Word that You
have not spoken in secret, from somewhere in
a land of darkness. You have not said to Jacob's
descendants, "Seek me in vain." You, Lord,
speak the truth. You declare what is right (Isa.
45:19).

Your Holy Spirit—the Spirit of truth—
will guide me into all truth. He will not speak
on His own. He will speak only what He hears
from You (John 16:13).

And as the Holy Spirit who dwells within
me searches and pinpoints areas of deception
in my life, give me sound discernment to understand as He guides me into all truth.

Thank You, faithful Father.

Walking with god in pursuit of daily obedience is the sure means of fulfilling each of his wonderful plans.

Glorious God, how I celebrate the fact that my eyes have never seen, my ears have never heard, and my mind has never conceived what You have prepared for me and all the others who truly love You. Help me also to understand that this awesome plan is revealed to me by Your Spirit (1 Cor. 2:9).

As surely as You convinced the apostle Paul, convince me thoroughly that neither death nor life, neither angels nor demons, neither the present nor the future, nor any powers, neither height nor depth, nor anything else in all creation, will be able to separate me from the love of God that is in Christ Jesus my Lord (Rom. 8:38–39).

WE TEND TO FORGET WHAT GOD HAS
DONE FOR US. WE THINK WE MUST
HAVE DONE SOMETHING RIGHT FOR
HIM TO HAVE BEEN SO GOOD TO US.

Lord God, I thank You for Your Word that assures me there is now no condemnation for those who are in Christ Jesus, because through Him the law of the Spirit of life has set me free from the law of sin and death (Rom. 8:1–2).

I praise You with all my soul, Lord, and I never want to forget all Your benefits. You are the One who forgives all my sins and heals my diseases, who redeems my life from the pit and crowns me with love and compassion, who satisfies my desires with good things so that my youth is renewed like the eagle's.

You, Lord, work righteousness and justice for all the oppressed (Ps. 103:2–6).

Obedience is not arriving at a perpetual state of godliness but perpetually following hard after God.

God, according to Your Word, blessed is the man who always fears the Lord, but he who hardens his heart falls into trouble (Prov. 28:14). Please make and keep my heart soft toward You!

Lord, Your Word says that he who trusts in himself is a fool, but he who walks in wisdom is kept safe (Prov. 28:26). I've come to realize that I cannot trust in myself. My safety is in learning to trust in You, Lord.

Cause my soul to yearn for You in the night and to long for You in the morning (Isa. 26:9). Transfer my yearning and longing to You, because You alone fill me in every way! Lord, You will never be a detriment to me!

EACH OF US HAS TO DECIDE WHETHER WE'RE GOING TO BELIEVE GOD'S WORD OR WE'RE GOING TO BELIEVE OUR EYES AND EMOTIONS.

Lord, though I live in the world, I do not wage war as the world does. The weapons I fight with are not the weapons of the world. On the contrary, they have the power to demolish strongholds.

Your power can demolish arguments and every pretension that sets itself up against the knowledge of You, God, and take captive every thought and make it obedient to Christ (2 Cor. 10:3–5).

Enable me, Lord! Help me not just to read it and say it, but to believe it and do it! You will rescue me from every evil attack and will bring me safely to Your heavenly kingdom. To You be glory forever (2 Tim. 4:18).

NEVER WILL HE HOLD YOUR HAND MORE TIGHTLY THAN WHEN HE IS LEADING YOU THROUGH THE DARK.

Father, You looked down from Your sanctuary on high, from heaven You viewed the earth, to hear the groans of the prisoners and release those who were condemned to death (Ps. 102:19–20).

Lord Jesus, in Your name and authority, I say to the devil, "Do not gloat over me, my enemy! Though I have fallen, I will rise. Though I sit in darkness, the Lord will be my light. I have sinned, but Christ bore my wrath on the cross. He pleads my case and establishes my right. He will bring me out into the light, and I will see his righteousness. Then you, my enemy, will see it and be covered with shame" (Mic. 7:8–10).

God's primary purpose in healing us from our hurts is to introduce us to new depths of relationship with himself.

Lord, in my heart I plan my course, but You determine my steps (Prov. 16:9).

Life is not going as I planned. But I am so grateful that You are not caught off guard. You knew everything that would befall me. So please direct my steps as You determine.

I need You, Lord.

Carry me when I cannot walk.

For though I walk in the midst of trouble, You preserve my life. Stretch out Your hand against the anger of my foes. With Your right hand, save me.

You will fulfill Your purpose for me. Your love, O Lord, endures forever. Do not abandon the works of Your hands (Ps. 138:7–8).

GOD LAVISHLY LOVES EVERY
PERSON, BUT HE RESERVES THE
RIGHT TO DEMONSTRATE HIS
LOVING MERCY TO THE OBEDIENT.

Lord, Your Word tells me that when I stand praying, if I hold anything against anyone, I am to forgive him or her, so that You, my Father in heaven, may forgive me my sins (Mark 11:25).

If I am offering my gifts to You through worship or service, and remember that my brother has something against me, I am to leave my gift there in front of the altar. I am to first go and be reconciled to my brother, then I am to come and offer my gift (Matt. 5:23–24).

Help me to be obedient to Your will. Forgive me my debts, Lord, as I also have forgiven my debtors (Matt. 6:12).

GOD OFFERS US THE DAILY TREASURE OF HIS STRENGTH, WISDOM, AND KNOWLEDGE, THE DAILY TREASURE OF HIS SURE FOUNDATION.

Father, like the Israelites, sometimes You speak to me through one of Your servants, but I do not listen because of my discouragement and cruel bondage (Exod. 6:9).

O Lord, help me listen to You, or I will never be free! Open my spiritual eyes and ears to see and hear the way to freedom. The unfolding of Your words gives light. It gives understanding to the simple (Ps. 119:130).

God, You who comfort the downcast, please comfort me by sending on of Your own to minister to me (2 Cor. 7:6), if indeed I will not become more dependent on him or her than on You.

I AM THANKFUL THAT GOD ALLOWS
DARKNESS TO FOLLOW REBELLION.
SOMETIMES HE USES DARKNESS TO
LEAD US TO THE LIGHT.

Father, according to Your Word, a person can be handed over to Satan, so that the sinful nature may be destroyed and his or her spirit saved on the day of the Lord (I Cor. 5:5).

O God, please help me not to continue to resist repentance and be handed over to Satan for a season. Help me to turn my life over to You now.

I admit that I reaped absolutely no benefit from the things I'm not ashamed of. Those things result in death. But now that I have been set free, the benefit I am reaping leads to holiness, and the result is eternal life. For the wages of sin is death, but the gift of God is eternal life in Christ Jesus my Lord (Rom. 6:21–23).

THE ENEMY KNOWS BETTER THAN WE DO THAT NOTHING IS BIGGER OR MORE POWERFUL THAN OUR GOD.

Lord God, I feel like the enemy has tracked me down. I feel as if he has tried to surround me, with eyes alert, to throw me to the ground. He is like a lion hungry for prey, like a great lion crouching in cover.

Rise up, O Lord, and confront him. Bring him down! Rescue me from his wickedness! (Ps. 17:11–13).

Look upon the enemy that oppresses me, and let smoke rise from Your nostrils! Let consuming fire come from Your mouth!

Part the heavens and come down! Mount the cherubim and fly! Soar on the wings of the wind! Shoot Your arrows, Lord, and scatter my enemy! (Ps. 18:8–10, 14).

WHAT A DISSERVICE WE DO WHEN
WE HUMANIZE GOD BY IMAGINING
HIM AS THE BEST OF HUMANITY
RATHER THAN ALL-TOGETHER GOD.

Lord God, You are very great. You are
clothed with splendor and majesty. You wrap
Yourself in light as with a garment. You stretch
out the heavens like a tent and lay the beams of
Your upper chambers on their waters.

You make the clouds Your chariot and ride
on the wings of the wind. You make the winds
Your messengers, flames of fire Your servants
(Ps. 104:1–4).

My Father and my God, You are seated on
a throne, high and exalted. The train of Your
robe fills the temple. Above You are the ser-
aphs, calling to one another, "Holy, holy, holy
is the Lord Almighty; the whole earth is full of
His glory" (Isa. 6:1–3).

OUR CALLINGS REMAIN A HOPE UNTIL
WE ALLOW THE EYES OF OUR HEARTS
TO BE ENLIGHTENED AND CHOOSE TO
ACCEPT THEM.

Father, in the parable of the sower, You teach us that the seed of Your Word that falls along the path represents the ones who hear, and the devil comes and takes away the word from their hearts, so that they may not believe (Luke 8:12). Lord, please help me to actively receive Your Word into my heart upon hearing it so that the devil cannot come and take it from me before it has time to take root.

I also pray that I will not be like those who receive the Word with joy when they hear it, but they have no root. They believe for a while, but in the time of testing they fall away (Luke 8:13). Help me to receive Your Word and hang on to it tightly.

A PRISONER UNAWARE IS THE KIND OF PRISONER MOST VULNERABLE TO HER CAPTORS, THE EASIEST PREY THERE IS.

Father, Your Word clearly states that You will punish the world for its evil, the wicked for their sins. You will put an end to the arrogance of the haughty and will humble the pride of the ruthless (Isa. 13:11).

Lord, even mighty King Nebuchadnezzar learned to praise and exalt and glorify the King of heaven and acknowledge that everything You do is right, that all Your ways are just, and that those who walk in pride, You are able to humble (Dan. 4:37).

Your Word says that pride hardens the heart (Dan. 5:20). Your desire for me is that I be tenderhearted (Eph. 4:32, KJV). Please melt any hardness in my heart.

HAVE YOU TOO QUICKLY DECIDED THAT WHAT YOU HAVE DONE OR WHAT YOU ARE DOING IS ALL YOU'LL EVER DO?

Father, You have said in Your Word, "Whoever invokes blessing in the land will do so by the God of truth; he who takes an oath in the land will swear by the God of truth. For the past troubles will be forgotten and hidden from my eyes" (Isa. 65:16).

Lord, I have plenty of past troubles. They seem to continue right before my eyes. Please, God of truth, invoke a blessing over my life and release me from my past.

I was once darkness, but now I am light in You. Help me to live as a child of light, for the fruit of the light consists in all goodness, righteousness, and truth. Help me to seek You and find what pleases You (Eph. 5:8–10).

APRIL

IF WE'RE WILLING TO ADMIT OUR LACK OF CONFIDENCE IN HIM, CHRIST IS MORE THAN WILLING TO HELP US OVERCOME OUR UNBELIEF.

Father, thank You for telling me that You Yourself express Your love uniquely to those who have loved Christ and believe He came from God (John 16:27).

And Lord Jesus, as hard as this is for me to fathom, Your Word says that just as Your Father has loved You, so You love me!

You love me so much that You want me to remain in Your love. If I obey Your commands, I will remain in Your love, just as You have obeyed Your Father's commands and remain in His love. You told me this so Your joy may be in me, and that my joy may be complete (John 15:9–11).

EVEN IF I BLOW IT, I CAN CHOOSE TO FOLLOW HIM THE REST OF THE WAY. IT'S NEVER TOO LATE TO START FOLLOWING HIS LEAD IN A CRISIS.

Lord God, I desire to claim the words Moses delivered to Your ancient people: Help me not to be afraid. Enable me to stand firm so I will see the deliverance that You, Lord, will bring me today.

You, Lord, will fight for me; help me only to be still (Exod. 14:13–14).

Father God, make me strong and courageous. Help me not to be afraid or terrified because of anyone else, for You go with me, Lord God. You will never leave me or forsake me (Deut. 31:6).

How I thank You for the assurance that You will not reject Your people. You will never forsake Your inheritance (Ps. 94:14).

IF WE ARE GOING TO LIVE IN FREEDOM, WE HAVE NO CHOICE BUT TO RENOUNCE EVERY SINGLE SECRET PLACE OF SIN IN OUR LIVES TO GOD.

O Lord our God, other lords besides You have ruled over me, but Your name alone is the one I want to honor (Isa. 26:13). Please help me understand that these sins and addictions have been terrible and destructive rulers in my life. Help me cease to honor them.

Help me see them like a bed too short to stretch out on and a blanket too narrow to wrap around me (Isa. 28:20). Help me accept the truth that the objects of my sinful desires are not enough!

Father, Your Word tells me that anyone who trusts in You will never be put to shame (Rom. 10:11). How I celebrate that the time has come to put all shame behind me!

Faith is god's invitation to make the impossible possible. He is glorified when we are enabled to do what we're unable to do.

I am Your dearly loved child. I am from You, Lord God, and have overcome the influences of the evil kingdom, because the One who is in me is greater than the one who is in the world (1 John 4:4).

You are the Lord, the God of all mankind. Nothing is too hard for You! (Jer. 32:27).

Now unto You who are able to do immeasurably more than all I ask or imagine, according to Your power that is at work within me, to You be the glory in the church and in Christ Jesus throughout all generations, forever and ever. Amen! (Eph. 3:20–21).

SATISFYING YOUR INNERMOST PLACES WITH JESUS IS A BENEFIT OF THE GLORIOUS COVENANT RELATIONSHIP YOU HAVE WITH GOD IN CHRIST.

In tears I have sought You, Lord God. I desire to come and bind myself to You in an everlasting covenant that will not be forgotten (Jer. 50:4–5).

Father, give me a heart to know You, that You are the Lord. I am Yours, and You are mine, for I have returned to You with all my heart (Jer. 24:7). You have said that if I will return to You, You will return to me, Lord God Almighty (Mal. 3:7).

Thank You for granting me repentance leading to a knowledge of the truth! Thank You for causing me to come to my senses and escape the trap of the devil, who had taken me captive to do his will (2 Tim. 2:25–26).

IF NOTHING FRIGHTENING EVER HAPPENED, HOW COULD THE ASSURANCE OF GOD'S CONSTANT PRESENCE BE THE QUIETER OF OUR FEARS?

Under the inspiration of the Holy Spirit, the writer of Psalm 119 said, "It was good for me to be afflicted, so that I might learn your decrees. The law from your mouth is more precious to me than thousands of pieces of silver and gold. Your hand made me and formed me; give me understanding to learn your commands. May those who fear you rejoice when they see me, for I have put my hope in your word" (Ps. 119:71–74).

I am only beginning to understand what he meant, Lord. We never know what You and Your Word mean until we are so afflicted that we cannot live without You. Teach me Your powerful Word, so that meaning can come forth from tragedy.

OBEDIENT LIVES FLOW FROM OBEDIENT DAYS, AND VICTORIOUS LIVES FLOW FROM VICTORIOUS DAYS.

Lord Jesus, when You were being led out to be executed, after being beaten, ridiculed, and spit upon, You said, "Father, forgive them, for they do not know what they are doing" (Luke 23:34).

If You can forgive those kinds of things by Your strength and power, being totally innocent, I can forgive the things that have been done to me. I also acknowledge that people who have hurt me throughout my life haven't always known what they were doing or what repercussions their actions would have.

You, Lord, are merciful and forgiving, even though I have rebelled against You (Dan. 9:9). Help me be merciful and forgiving to others.

No matter how I have reacted to betrayal or any other kind of heartbreak, I am glad to know a way exists to be victorious.

Father, even the great apostle Paul did not want us to be uninformed about the hardships he suffered while in the province of Asia. He, too, was under great pressure, far beyond his ability to endure, so that he despaired even of life (2 Cor. 1:8).

Even many of Your mightiest servants have despaired of life. Like them, however, I must stand once again in Your strength and courage and allow You to pour Your life back into me.

Victorious Lord, how I thank You that the oppressor will come to an end, and destruction will cease. The aggressor will vanish from the land (Isa. 16:4).

We're far more likely to act like the old man of sin when we still feel like the old man of sin.

Lord, if I remain stubborn and unrepentant in heart, Your Word says I am storing up wrath for myself for the day of Your wrath, when Your righteous judgment will be revealed. For those who are self-seeking, reject the truth, and follow evil, there will be wrath and anger. There will be trouble and distress for every human being who does evil . . . but glory, honor, and peace for everyone who does good (Rom. 2:5–10).

Help me to see that the "good" You want me to do in response to my sin is to repent and receive Your help, to turn my life entirely over to You. I do not have to settle for a life hopelessly entangled in sin. Set me free, Lord.

THE ENEMY KNOWS THE POWER OF PRAYER. HE'S BEEN WATCHING IT FURIOUSLY FOR THOUSANDS OF YEARS.

The Lord lives! Praise be to my Rock! Exalted be God my Savior! You are the God who avenges me, who subdues and saves me from my enemy. Therefore, I will praise You among the nations, O Lord. I will sing praises to Your name. You give great victories, Lord God. You show unfailing kindness to Your anointed ones (Ps. 18:46–50).

In the day of trouble, keep me safe in Your dwelling. Hide me in the shelter of Your tabernacle and set me high upon a rock. Cause my head to be exalted above the enemy surrounding me. Then remind me to offer You the sacrifice of praise with shouts of joy, and help me to sing and make music to You! (Ps. 27:5–6).

Christ isn't asking us to believe in our ability to exercise unwavering faith. He is asking us to believe that He is able.

My Father, great are Your works! They are pondered by all who delight in them. Glorious and majestic are Your deeds, O Lord, and Your righteousness endures forever.

You have caused Your many wonders to be remembered; You are gracious and compassionate. The works of Your hands are faithful and just; all Your precepts are trustworthy. They are steadfast for ever and ever, done in faithfulness and uprightness (Ps. 111:2–4, 7–8).

For me, there is but one God, the Father, from whom all things came and for whom I live; and there is but one Lord, Jesus Christ, through whom all things came and through whom we live (1 Cor. 8:6).

IF YOU DARE TO BELIEVE
AND DON'T GET YOUR MIRACLE,
GOD HAS A GREATER ONE PLANNED.
STAY TUNED.

Jesus, You told Your close followers, who were taught how to seek the Father's heart, that whatever they asked for in prayer they were to believe they received it and it would be theirs (Mark 11:24). O Father, help me to know Your heart intimately so that I'll know how to pray, what to pray, and believe in advance that I will receive it!

Please help me not to be foolish and slow of heart (Luke 24:25). If You speak to me regarding earthly things and I do not believe, how then will I believe when You speak of heavenly things? (John 3:12).

Help me to believe You here and now and not just in things concerning heaven. You are God of heaven and earth!

FAITHFULNESS IN OUR CHRISTIAN
WALK REQUIRES ORDER, BUT WITHIN
THAT ORDER IS GLORIOUS ROOM FOR
COLOR AND CREATIVITY.

My Father, I celebrate the fact that You,
Jehovah God, take delight in Your people; You
crown the humble with salvation (Ps. 149:4).
Even those who have been forsaken and hated
by the world, You can make them the everlasting pride and the joy of all generations (Isa.
60:15). Your approval and opinion are all that
really matter.

Your Word teaches that You humble and
test Your children so that in the end it might go
well with us (Deut. 8:16). You do not humble
and test us to bring us low and cause us to fail
but to teach us how to succeed in You. How I
thank You that the humble will rejoice in the
Lord; the needy will rejoice in the Holy One
of Israel (Isa. 29:19).

When we turn away to other gods, we often force God to hold back his blessing and stop his giving hand.

O Lord, Your Word says Your eyes constantly look for truth. When You chastised the children of Israel, You struck them, but they felt no pain; You crushed them, but they refused correction. They made their faces harder than stone and refused to repent (Jer. 5:3).

Lord God, have mercy on me. Help me not to be unresponsive to Your correction. You only chastise in love in order to bring me back to the place of safety . . . to You, Lord God.

Help me not hide behind lies. When You look for truth, I pray You will find truth in me, for Your inspired Word declares that the knowledge of Your truth leads to godliness (Titus 1:1).

WE CAN ENJOY GOD'S PRESENCE
EVEN WHEN LIFE IS NOT ENJOYABLE,
BUT WE MUST FIRST ACCEPT HIS
PRESENCE AS AN ABSOLUTE FACT.

Because of Your great love for me, You, God, who are rich in mercy, made me alive with Christ even when I was dead in transgressions—it is by grace I have been saved.

You raised me up with Christ and seated me with Him in the heavenly realms in Christ Jesus, in order that in the coming ages You might show the incomparable riches of Your grace, expressed in Your kindness to me in Christ Jesus (Eph. 2:4–7).

Great is Your love toward me, O Lord. Your faithfulness endures forever (Ps. 117:2). Set my heart at rest in Your presence when my heart wants to condemn me. For You, God, are greater than my heart, and You know everything (1 John 3:19–20).

THE BETTER WE KNOW GOD, THE MORE WE TRUST HIM. THE MORE WE TRUST HIM, THE MORE WE SENSE HIS PEACE WHEN THE COLD WIND BLOWS.

Lord God, I revel in Your promise that You will go before me and make the rough places smooth; You will shatter the doors of bronze and cut through their iron bars.

And You will give me the treasures of darkness, the hidden wealth of secret places, in order that I may know that it is You, the Lord, the God of Israel, who calls me by my name (Isa. 45:2–3, NASB).

My Lord, You are a refuge for the oppressed, a stronghold in times of trouble. Those who know Your name will trust in You, for You, Lord, have never forsaken those who seek You (Ps. 9:9–10). O Lord, I do know Your name. Please swell my trust in You.

WITHOUT THE POTTER, CLAY IS JUST DIRT. WHEN WE SEEK TO PLEASE HIM, HE SEEKS TO PERFECT US, AND LIFE WORKS.

Merciful God, I have learned the hard way that nothing good lives in me, that is, in my sinful nature. For I have the desire to do what is good, but I cannot carry it out (Rom. 7:18). But in You I have all the power I need! You've given me the treasure of the Holy Spirit who lives in this weak jar of clay to show that this all-surpassing power is from God and not from me! (2 Cor. 4:7).

Father of mercies, no matter what I've done or how long I've done it, there is no condemnation for those who are in Christ Jesus, because through Christ Jesus the law of the Spirit of life set me free from the law of sin and death (Rom. 8:1–2). Hallelujah! Help me to fully accept this truth.

THE SPIRIT OF GOD RELEASED
THROUGH OUR PRAYERS AND
THE PRAYERS OF OTHERS TURNS
COWARDS INTO CONQUERORS.

Lord, I can find great encouragement in knowing that many believers, weak in their natural selves, have walked faithfully and victoriously with You (Heb. 11).

Therefore, since I am surrounded by such a great cloud of witnesses, help me throw off everything that hinders and the sin that so easily entangles, and help me run with perseverance the race marked out for me.

Help me fix my eyes on Jesus, the author and perfecter of my faith, who for the joy set before Him endured the cross, scorning its shame, and sat down at the right hand of Your throne, O God (Heb. 12:1–2).

THE GREATEST JOY IN OUR LIVES IS THE VERY THING WE HAVE DESERVED THE LEAST. IT IS AN ABSOLUTE GIFT OF GRACE.

Father, how I thank You that Your servants were also sinners saved by grace. The apostle Paul said, "I thank Christ Jesus our Lord, who has given me strength, that he considered me faithful, appointing me to his service." Even though he was once a blasphemer and a persecutor and a violent man, he was shown mercy.

Like him, Lord, Your grace has been poured out on me abundantly, along with the faith and love that are in Christ Jesus (1 Tim. 1:12–14). Never let me show contempt for the riches of Your kindness, tolerance, and patience, not realizing that Your kindness leads me toward repentance (Rom. 2:4).

IT'S NOT ALL SMALL STUFF. WE FACE A LOT OF BIG STUFF OUT THERE. AND ONLY THROUGH PRAYER ARE WE WASHED IN PEACE.

You are forgiving and good, O Lord, abounding in love to all who call to You. Hear my prayer, O Lord; listen to my cry for mercy. In the day of my trouble I will call to You, for You will answer me (Ps. 86:5–7).

Yet You are always with me; You hold me by my right hand. You guide me with Your counsel, and afterward You will take me into glory. Whom have I in heaven but You? And earth has nothing I desire besides You. My flesh and my heart may fail, but You, God, are the strength of my heart and my portion forever.

As for me, it is good to be near You, Sovereign Lord. I have made You my refuge; I will tell of all Your deeds (Ps. 73:23–26, 28).

A LIFESTYLE OF BELIEVING GOD MAKES YOU BOLDER IN YOUR LOVE FOR OTHERS AND IN WHAT YOU CAN BELIEVE GOD FOR IN THEIR LIVES.

Your Word asks me why I judge or look down on my brother. I acknowledge to You today, Lord, that we will all stand before Your judgment seat.

It is written: "As surely as I live," says the Lord, "every knee will bow before me; every tongue will confess to God." So then, each of us will give an account of himself to God.

Therefore help me stop passing judgment on others. Instead, I make up my mind not to put any stumbling block or obstacle in my brother's way (Rom. 14:10–13).

Lord, You have extended such grace to me. You have forgiven my wickedness and remembered my sins no more (Heb. 8:12). Help me express the same grace toward others.

PURE APPRECIATION FOR HIS PRESENCE EMERGES FROM THE DAILY WALK, PERHAPS IN THE MUNDANE MORE THAN THE MIRACULOUS.

Lord, according to Your Word, if my eyes are bad, my whole body will be full of darkness. If then the light within me is darkness, how great is that darkness! (Matt. 6:23).

Lord, this verse tells me that the focus of my gaze, where my eyes are fixed, has a monumental impact on whether light or darkness will be prevalent in my life. Please, Lord, heal my eyes—my sight!—that I might look to You, my Hope and my Redeemer.

Lord, even though I may feel covered in darkness, even the darkness will not be dark to You; the night will shine like the day, for darkness is as light to You (Ps. 139:12). Cloak me in Your presence, God, for in You is no darkness at all.

WE WILL NEVER TAKE OUR PLACES AS "MORE THAN OVERCOMERS" WITH NOTHING TO OVERCOME.

Lord, as I approach You with repentance and the desire to live differently, who is he that condemns? You, Christ Jesus, who died—more than that, who was raised to life—are at the right hand of God and You are interceding for me! No, in all these things I will be more than a conqueror through You who loves me (Rom. 8:33–34, 37).

Your Word says that I have been made holy through the sacrifice of Christ's body. This means I have been set apart for sacred use rather than common use. Yes, I will be tempted at times to think like the unholy person I used to be (Heb. 10:10). But keep me on track. Help me not to call anything impure that You have made clean (Acts 10:15).

THE ENEMY IS CONSTANTLY TRYING TO CONVINCE US THAT THE CHRISTIAN LIFE IS SACRIFICIAL AT BEST AND ARTIFICIAL AT WORST.

You, Lord, are my light and my salvation—whom shall I fear? You, Lord, are the stronghold of my life—of whom shall I be afraid?

When evil advances against me to devour my flesh, when my enemy and my foe attacks me, cause him to stumble and fall. Though an unseen army besiege me, cause my heart not to fear; though war break out against me, even then will I be confident.

Because one thing I ask of, You, Lord, this is what I seek: that I may dwell in Your house all the days of my life, to gaze upon Your beauty and to seek You in Your temple (Ps. 27:1–4).

REMEMBERING WHAT GOD HAS DONE IN THE PAST SPILLS OVER INTO BELIEVING GOD FOR OUR FUTURE.

My Lord and my God, it is You who measured the waters in the hollow of Your hand, and with the breadth of Your hand marked off the heavens (Isa. 40:12). You sit enthroned above the circle of the earth, and its people are like grasshoppers. You stretch out the heavens like a canopy, and spread them out like a tent to live in (Isa. 40:22).

O Lord, help me to lift my eyes and look to the heavens and acknowledge who created all these. You bring out the starry host one by one, and call each of them by name. Because of Your great power and mighty strength, not one of them is missing (Isa. 40:26).

O Father, how I thank You that my help comes from You, the Maker of heaven and earth (Ps. 121:2).

LOVE OTHERS NOT BY TRYING TO BECOME THEIR GOD BUT BY FUELING THEIR OWN FAITH IN GOD.

Father, according to Your Word, those who heard the testimony of the woman at the well said, "We no longer believe just because of what you said; now we have heard for ourselves, and we know that this man really is the Savior of the world" (John 4:42). Please cause my life to impact others by making them desire to meet You for themselves and believe!

O Lord, I want others to be able to boast to You about my perseverance and faith in any persecutions and trials I endure (2 Thess. 1:4). Help me to remember that others observe the way I handle trials. I want to have a faithful witness, Lord. Like Timothy's grandmother, Lois, and his mother, Eunice, help me to pass down a heritage of faith (2 Tim. 1:5).

THE CHURCH HERSELF IS THE ONLY TRUE FOE IN THE WAR OF REVIVAL; HER PRIDE ALONE PREVAILS AGAINST HER.

Father, You have promised that if Your people, who are called by Your name, will humble themselves and pray and seek Your face and turn from their wicked ways, then will You hear from heaven and will forgive their sin and will heal their land (2 Chron. 7:14).

Please help me to understand that corporate revival begins with personal, individual revival. Help me to humble myself and pray and seek Your face and turn from my own wicked ways, to understand when the pride in my heart is deceiving me (Jer. 49:16).

Thank You, Lord, for hearing me from heaven and forgiving my sin and bringing healing to my heart.

THE ENEMY IS HOPING WE'D RATHER REMAIN IN DENIAL THAN LET GOD'S WORD PENETRATE OUR LIVES AND SET US FREE.

Lord God, I do not want You to have to say of me, "This child has not obeyed the Lord her God or responded to correction. Truth has perished; it has vanished from her lips" (Jer. 7:28). Lord, if I allow truth to perish in my life and never return to it, I will be held in bondage the rest of my days.

Savior and Lord, You are my way. You are my truth. You are my life. You are my only means of going to the Father (John 14:6).

Thank You for the access You afforded me when You laid down Your life in my place. Help me to give You great joy by walking in the truth, just as You commanded us (2 John 4).

SOMETIMES GOD REQUIRES US TO FOLLOW A FAIR AMOUNT OF REPETITION FOR A LONG TIME UNTIL HE DEEMS A SEASON COMPLETE.

Lord, my God, You long to be gracious to me; You rise to show me compassion. For You, Lord, are a God of justice. Blessed are all who wait for You!

We the people of God, will one day weep no more. How gracious You will be when I cry for help! As soon as You hear, You will answer me.

Although You, Lord, have at times given me the bread of adversity and the water of affliction, my teachers will one day be hidden no more; with my own eyes I will see them. Whether I turn to the right or to the left, my ears will hear a voice behind me, saying, "This is the way; walk in it" (Isa. 30:18–21).

EVERY DAY CAN BRING TROUBLE,
BUT WE HAVE A BLESSED TROUBLE-
SHOOTER. WE MUST DAILY SET OUR
FACE ON THE FACE OF CHRIST.

You, O God, do see trouble and grief; You consider it to take it in hand. The victim commits himself to You; You are the helper of the fatherless (Ps. 10:14).

O God, help me to understand that I am no longer a victim of anyone else's misuse or rejection when I commit myself entirely to You. Make me a victor, Lord Jesus!

The wicked lie in wait for the righteous, seeking their very lives; but You, Lord, will not leave them in their power or let them be condemned when brought to trial.

Your instruction to me is to wait for You and keep Your way. You will exalt Your own to inherit the land; when the wicked are cut off, we will see it (Ps. 37:32–34).

MAY

CHRIST SETS US FREE BY THE POWER
OF HIS SPIRIT. HE MAINTAINS OUR
FREEDOM AS WE LEARN TO LIVE FROM
DAY TO DAY IN HIS POWER.

God, I claim Your Word that says I did not receive a spirit that makes me a slave again to fear, but I received the Spirit of sonship. And by Him I cry, "Abba, Father" (Rom. 8:15). Help me to cry out unashamedly to You, my Father, when I am gripped by fear. This kind of fear is not of You! (2 Tim. 1:7).

Victorious God, I thank You that the weapons with which I fight are not the weapons of the world. On the contrary, they have divine power to demolish strongholds. I demolish arguments and every pretension that sets itself up against the knowledge of God, and I choose to take captive every thought to make it obedient to Christ! (2 Cor. 10:4–5).

WHEN WAS THE LAST TIME YOU FELT LIKE EVERYTHING IN YOUR LIFE WAS QUAKING EXCEPT YOUR STABILITY IN CHRIST?

By faith Abraham, when called to go to a place he would later receive as his inheritance, obeyed and went, even though he did not know where he was going (Heb. 11:8).

Lord, help me to be willing to follow You in obedience even when I'm not sure where I'm heading. Your divine power has given me everything I need for life and godliness through my knowledge of You who called me by Your own glory and goodness (2 Pet. 1:3).

You, Lord, will guide me always; You will satisfy my needs in a sun-scorched land and will strengthen my frame. I will be like a well-watered garden, like a spring whose waters never fail (Isa. 58:11).

GOD LOOKS UPON OUR HEARTS AND KNOWS WHETHER WE HAVE ANY AUTHENTIC DESIRE TO BE DIFFERENT OR IF WE'RE ALL TALK.

Father, how I praise You for exalting Christ to Your own right hand as Prince and Savior that He might give repentance and forgiveness of sins to Your people! (Acts 5:31). Your Word says that if Your people will turn, each of us, from our evil practices, we can stay in the land You have given us (Jer. 25:5).

Lord, I have examined my ways and tested them, and returned wholeheartedly to You (Lam. 3:40). Search me, O God, and know my heart; test me and know my anxious thoughts. See if there is any offensive way in me and lead me in the way everlasting (Ps. 139:23–24). And if in examining myself, I have overlooked sin, please show me and lead me to full repentance and restoration!

FEW PEOPLE HAVE GRATEFUL HEARTS LIKE CAPTIVES WHO HAVE BEEN FREED AND THE AFFLICTED WHO HAVE BEEN HEALED.

I love You, Lord, for You heard my voice; You heard my cry for mercy. Because You turned Your ear to me, I will call on You as long as I live.

The cords of death entangled me, the anguish of the grave came upon me; I was overcome by trouble and sorrow. Then I called on the name of the Lord: O Lord, save me!

You, Lord, are gracious and righteous; my God is full of compassion. You, Lord, protect the simple-hearted; when I was in great need, You saved me.

Be at rest once more, O my soul, for the Lord has been good to you (Ps. 116:1–7). I choose to cast my cares on You, Lord, and You will sustain me (Ps. 55:22).

LOVE IS NOT A SPIRITUAL GIFT.
OTHERWISE WE'D ALL CONVENIENTLY
CLAIM NOT TO POSSESS IT. RATHER,
LOVE IS A PRIORITY CALLING.

Lord, I have heard that it was said, "Love your neighbor and hate your enemy." But You tell me to love my enemies and pray for those who persecute me, that I might be a child of my Father in heaven (Matt. 5:43–44).

Father God, if I love those who love me, what reward will I get? Are not even the godless doing that? And if I greet only those to whom I am close, what am I doing more than others? Do not even pagans do that? (Matt. 5:46–47).

You have called me to be different, Lord! You have called me to go far beyond the actions of even the noblest pagan. Help me not to be overcome by evil but to overcome evil with good (Rom. 12:21).

GOD'S LIGHT WILL ALWAYS LEAD US RIGHT BACK TO THE PATH. NO MATTER HOW LONG THE DETOUR HAS BEEN, RETURN IS ONLY A SHORTCUT AWAY.

Lord, when the Israelites heard Your voice out of the darkness, while the mountain was ablaze with fire, all the leading men of their tribes and their elders came forward (Deut. 5:23). Please help me to hear Your voice out of my darkness and come to You, Lord.

Lord, Your servant Job felt he was in the land of deepest night, of deep shadow and disorder, where even the light is like darkness (Job 10:22). You restored someone who knew a much bleaker darkness than mine. You will restore me, too, if I will let You.

You are my lamp, O Lord; You, the Lord, turn my darkness into light (2 Sam. 22:29). You, O Lord, keep my lamp burning; my God turns my darkness into light (Ps. 18:28).

What victory the enemy has in winning us over to prayerlessness. He would rather we do anything than pray.

My merciful God, since I have been raised with Christ, set my heart on things above, where Christ is seated at the right hand of God. Help me set my mind on things above, not on earthly things (Col. 3:1).

Lord, please take my passions and redirect them first and foremost toward You. Be the chief focus of all my passions and create a new heart within me with healthy emotions.

Father God, please help me not to shy away from praying to You. Your Word tells me to pray about everything! (Phil. 4:6). Help me to trust You and pour out my heart to You because You are my refuge (Ps. 62:8). You will not shame me or turn Your back on me. You want to help me overcome every stronghold.

The enemy knows we will be too handicapped to live in consistent victory until we actively believe we are who God says we are.

Praise be to You, the Lord my Rock, who trains my hands for war, my fingers for battle. You are my loving God and my fortress, my stronghold and my deliverer, my shield, in whom I take refuge.

Part Your heavens, O Lord, and come down; touch the mountains, so that they smoke. Send forth lightning and scatter the enemy; shoot Your arrows and rout them. Reach down Your hand from on high; deliver me and rescue me! (Ps. 144:1–2, 5–7).

Father God, I pray that You will cause no weapon forged against me to prevail. Enable me to refute the tongue of my accuser. Thank You for giving this as a heritage to Your servants, O Lord (Isa. 54:17).

WE CANNOT TAME THE LION OF JUDAH. THERE IS A MYSTERY, A WONDER, EVEN A WILDNESS ABOUT GOD WE CANNOT TAKE FROM HIM.

O, Father, I confess that I cannot fathom Your mysteries. I cannot probe Your limits, Almighty One. They are higher than the heavens. They are deeper than the depths of the grave. Their measure is longer than the earth and wider than the sea (Job 11:7–9).

To the Israelites, Lord, Your glory looked like a consuming fire on top of the mountain (Exod. 24:17). Help me to be thankful and to worship You acceptably with reverence and awe, because You, my God, are a consuming fire (Heb. 12:28–29).

Truly, You are both a God nearby and a God far away. No one can hide in secret places so that You cannot see him. You fill heaven and earth! (Jer. 23:23–24).

IF YOU PRAY THAT GOD WILL MOVE A MOUNTAIN AND HE DOESN'T, ASSUME CHRIST WANTS YOU TO CLIMB IT INSTEAD AND SEE HIM TRANSFIGURED.

God, please don't let me be the kind of person to whom You can say, "Unless you see miraculous signs and wonders, you will never believe" (John 4:48). Help me to respond to Your Son according to Your Word: "I believe and know that You are the Holy One of God" (John 6:69).

Christ Jesus, You said to Thomas, "Put your finger here; see my hands. Reach out your hand and put it into my side. Stop doubting and believe" (John 20:27). Lord, I cannot see Your visible hands, but if I'm willing to really look, I can see the visible evidences of Your invisible hands. Help me to cease being obstinate, refusing to believe. When I do this, I am maligning Your way (Acts 19:9).

CAN YOU ADMIT THAT SOME OF YOUR ATTEMPTS AT HUMILITY HAVE BEEN DRIVEN BY PRIDE?

God, in my pursuit to be free of pride, never let me delight in false humility. Help me not to be the kind of person who goes into great detail about what he has seen, and whose unspiritual mind puffs him up with idle notions (Col. 2:18). Your Word teaches that false humility and harsh treatment of the body lack any value in restraining sensual indulgence (Col. 2:23).

Instead, God, as one of Your chosen people, holy and dearly loved, help me to clothe myself with compassion, kindness, humility, gentleness, and patience (Col. 3:12). Help me to slander no one, to be peaceable and considerate, and to show true humility toward all men (Titus 3:2).

BECAUSE ONLY CHRIST CAN SET US
FREE, ALL OTHER GODS OR IDOLS——
ANYTHING WE USE AS A REPLACEMENT
FOR GOD——CAN ONLY ENSLAVE.

Merciful God, according to Your Word, everyone who does evil hates the light, and will not come into the light for fear that his deeds will be exposed. But whoever lives by the truth comes into the light, so that it may be seen plainly that what he has done has been done through God (John 3:20–21).

O God, help me to not be afraid to let You shine Your light on my darkness. Please cause Your light to permeate, expose, and treat any darkness or deception in me so that I can live freely in Your light!

Help me never to exchange the truth of God for a lie (Rom. 1:25). If any area remains in my life where I have made such a tragic exchange, reveal it and set me free.

GOD'S UNFAILING LOVE EXTENDS TO
THE MOST REBELLIOUS CAPTIVES AND
AFFLICTED FOOLS, THOSE WHO'VE
CRIED OUT TO HIM IN TROUBLE.

My Savior, Jesus Christ, Your Word says that greater love has no one than this, that he lay down his life for his friends (John 15:13). You have demonstrated the greatest act of friendship in my behalf that exists.

I praise You and thank You, Lord, for not treating me as my sins deserve or repaying me according to my iniquities. For as high as the heavens are above the earth, so great is Your love for those who fear You; as far as the east is from the west, so far have You removed my transgressions from me (Ps. 103:10–12).

Lord, You are good and Your love endures forever; Your faithfulness continues through all generations (Ps. 100:5).

ABIDING IN CHRIST IS THE KEY TO STAYING DELIBERATELY CONNECTED WITH OUR UPLAND SOURCE.

Father, before Your Son was taken away for trial and crucifixion, He shared His heart for us in a deep intercessory prayer. He wants those You have given Him to be with Him where He is, and to see His glory, the glory You have given Him because You loved Him before the creation of the world.

Lord God, Your Son came to make You known to me, and He will continue to make You known in order that the love You have for Him may be in us and that Jesus Himself may be in us (John 17:24–26). No matter how I may encounter rejection in the world around me, I am welcomed to abide in the Creator of heaven and earth and the perfect Son of the Most High God.

OUR PROMISED LANDS ARE CHARACTERIZED BY THE PRESENCE OF VICTORY, NOT THE ABSENCE OF OPPOSITION.

Father, Your Word promises we can know that in all things God works for the good of those who love Him, who have been called according to His purpose (Rom. 8:28).

My own problems and situations are not exempt from this list! As hard as it may be for me to comprehend, You can and will work these terrible challenges for good if I will cooperate with You and see myself as one called according to Your purpose.

Thanks be to You, my God, who always leads me in triumphal procession in Christ, desiring to spread everywhere through me the fragrance of the knowledge of Him! (2 Cor. 2:14). You only lead to victory, Christ Jesus. If I will keep following You, I'll get there.

EACH OF US MUST DECIDE WHERE WE'RE GOING TO PUT OUR ENERGY WHEN THE BATTLE GROWS FIERCE.

In a race all the runners run, but only one gets the prize. Lord, help me to run in such a way as to get the prize (I Cor. 9:24).

God, I do not consider myself yet to have taken hold of it. But one thing I do: Forgetting what is behind and straining toward what is ahead, I press on toward the goal to win the prize for which You have called me heavenward in Christ Jesus (Phil. 3:13–14). Help me to forget all past failures—or even achievements—and to focus on pressing forward with You now.

God of hope, I pray that You fill me with all joy and peace as I trust in You, so that I may overflow with hope by the power of the Holy Spirit (Rom. 15:13).

GOD SENDS HIS WORD FORTH, AND IT NEVER RETURNS VOID, UNCHAINING THE SOUL OF EVERY PERSON WITH THE COURAGE TO BELIEVE IT.

Lord, I echo the words of the apostle Paul who said, "Here is a trustworthy saying that deserves full acceptance: Christ Jesus came into the world to save sinners—of whom I am the worst. But for that very reason I was shown mercy so that in me, the worst of sinners, Christ Jesus might display his unlimited patience as an example for those who would believe on him and receive eternal life. Now to the King eternal, immortal, invisible, the only God, be honor and glory for ever and ever. Amen" (I Tim. 1:15–17).

Lord, even if I were the very worst of sinners—as sometimes I feel I am—You still forgive and are willing to use those who put their trust in You! Thank You, God!

IF WHAT YOU DESPERATELY NEED OR DEEPLY DESIRE IS FOUNDED IN THE WORD OF GOD, DON'T LET ANYONE TELL YOU THAT GOD CAN'T.

May Your unfailing love be my comfort, according to Your promise to Your servant. Let Your compassion come to me that I may live, for Your law is my delight. My soul faints with longing for Your salvation, but I have put my hope in Your Word (Ps. 119:76–77, 81).

My God is in heaven; He does whatever pleases Him (Ps. 115:3). Lord, sometimes my only answer will be that You are sovereign. Your Word says that the death of Your saints is absolutely precious to You (Ps. 116:15).

One day I will have all the answers. But until then, I must trust that You have power and dominion over all things and that You know best. Help me to believe this even when I don't feel this.

CAPTIVES TRULY SET FREE ARE THE
MOST COMPASSIONATE PEOPLE IN THE
WORLD. THEY DON'T SEE OTHERS
AS LESS THAN THEMSELVES.

If You, O Lord, kept a record of sin, who could stand? But with You there is forgiveness; therefore You are feared (Ps. 130:4). Lord, after all You've done for me and after all the sin You've forgiven in my life, help me to have so much fear and reverence for You that I will not withhold forgiveness from others.

Lord, I will not say to a person who has hurt me, "I'll pay you back for this wrong!" I will wait for You, Lord, and You will deliver me (Prov. 20:22). I will not say of someone who has wronged me, "I'll do to him as he has done to me; I'll pay that man back for what he did" (Prov. 24:29). Lord, give me more grace (James 4:6) so that I may increasingly extend it to others.

OUR HEARTBREAKS REALLY AREN'T ANYONE ELSE'S RESPONSIBILITY. THEY ARE CHRIST'S. REMEMBER, HE CAME TO BIND UP THE BROKENHEARTED.

Father, I am struggling. I feel that You have taken my companions and loved ones from me; the darkness is my closest friend. Lord, show me wonders in this place of darkness and reveal to me Your righteousness in this land of oblivion. Let them draw me to your light (Ps. 88:12, 18). Please come and rescue me. Be my closest companion and my dearest loved one.

Listen to my cry, for I am in desperate need; rescue me from those who pursue me, for they are too strong for me (Ps. 142:6). Lord, an important part of my victory will be admitting that without Your complete intervention, my oppressor is too strong for me. I am unable to be victorious without You.

THE ENEMY'S HOPE FOR CHRISTIANS IS THAT WE WILL EITHER BE SO INEFFECTIVE WE HAVE NO TESTIMONY, OR WE'LL RUIN THE ONE WE HAVE.

According to Your Word, a man's ways are in full view of the Lord, and You examine all our paths. The evil deeds of a wicked man ensnare him; the cord of his sin holds him fast. He will die for a lack of discipline, led astray by his own great folly (Prov. 5:21–23).

Lord, self-discipline is a fruit of the Spirit. Please fill me with Your Spirit and empower me with a self-discipline only You can give (Gal. 5:22–23).

God, please help me to love You with my whole heart, soul, mind, and strength, for this is Your priority for my life (Mark 12:30).Break my heart when I even think of doing what is dishonorable, Lord.

OUR NEED FOR DELIVERANCE
DOESN'T END ONCE WE BECOME
CHRISTIANS. WE STILL NEED LOTS OF
HELP AVOIDING SNARES AND PITFALLS.

Father God, according to Your Word, the wicked lie in wait for the righteous, seeking their very lives; but You will not leave them in their power or let them be condemned when brought to trial (Ps. 37:32–33).

O Lord, You have seen this; be not silent. Do not be far from me, O Lord. Awake, and rise to my defense! Contend for me, my God and my Lord. Vindicate me in Your righteousness, O Lord my God; do not let them gloat over me (Ps. 35:22–24).

Lord God, You are my stronghold in time of trouble. Help me and deliver me; deliver me from the wicked and save me, because I take refuge in You (Ps. 37:39–40).

UNLIKE PEOPLE, CHRIST IS NEVER INTIMIDATED BY THE DEPTH OF OUR NEED AND THE DEMONSTRATION OF OUR WEAKNESS.

You, my Lord, are the everlasting God, the Creator of the ends of the earth. You will not grow tired or weary, and Your understanding no one can fathom. You give strength to the weary and increase the power of the weak.

Even youths grow tired and weary, and young men stumble and fall; but when I hope in You, O, Lord, my strength will be renewed. I will soar on wings like eagles; I will run and not grow weary, I will walk and not faint (Isa. 40:28–31).

Ah, Sovereign Lord, You have made the heavens and the earth by Your great power and outstretched arm. Nothing is too hard for You! (Jer. 32:17).

FAITH IS THE ONLY THING THAT WILL EVER CLOSE THE GAP BETWEEN OUR THEOLOGY AND OUR REALITY.

Father, You've told me that when I ask I am to believe and not doubt, because he who doubts is like a wave of the sea, blown and tossed by the wind (James 1:6). You said to Your children, "If you do not stand firm in your faith, you will not stand at all" (Isa. 7:9). Please teach me to stand firm, Lord.

Christ Jesus, before You rebuked the winds and the waves, You asked Your disciples, "You of little faith, why are you so afraid?" (Matt. 8:26). Help me to fully embrace that the One whom the winds and waves obey is the same One who watches over me. Help me not to hinder Your works on my behalf over a lack of faith.

LIFE VASTLY SIMPLIFIES, AND
SATISFACTION GREATLY AMPLIFIES
WHEN WE BEGIN TO REALIZE OUR
AWESOME ROLES——THAT GOD IS GOD.

Sovereign Lord, Your Word says, "This is the one I esteem: he who is humble and contrite in spirit, and trembles at my word" (Isa. 66:2). Father, I can hardly imagine being someone You esteem, but I sincerely want to be! Make me that kind of person through the power of Your Holy Spirit, Lord.

You said to Your servant, Daniel, "Since the first day that you set your mind to gain understanding and to humble yourself before your God, your words were heard, and I have come in response to them" (Dan. 10:12).

You are my God just as You were his. If I set my mind to gain understanding and to humble myself before You, You will hear my words and come in response to them.

DO NOT ALLOW THE ENEMY ANOTHER SUCCESS AT USING YOUR PAST RECORD AGAINST YOU. GOD SAID HE IS DOING A NEW THING IN YOU.

Lord God, You have told us in Your Word that the devil was a murderer from the beginning, not holding to the truth, for there is no truth in him. When he lies, he speaks his native language, for he is a liar and the father of lies (John 8:44).

Father, please help me discern that wherever deception exists, the devil is at work. When I sin against You and choose to walk in deception rather than truth, please send others to gently instruct and confront me. Grant me repentance leading me to a knowledge of the truth (2 Tim. 2:25).

Never allow me to be one who is always learning but never able to acknowledge the truth (2 Tim. 3:7).

GOD DID NOT DESIGN US TO BOSS
OURSELVES. HE FORMED US TO
REQUIRE AUTHORITY SO WE'D LIVE IN
THE SAFETY OF HIS CAREFUL RULE.

My Jesus, according to Your Word, who-ever has Your commands and obeys them, he is the one who loves You. He who loves You will be loved by Your Father, and You too will love him and show Yourself to him (John 14:21). O God, please help me to live obediently and have the joy of seeing You revealed in all sorts of marvelous ways.

O Christ, cause Your love to absolutely compel me. Help me to be convinced that be-cause One died for all, therefore all died. Help me to realize and fully appreciate the fact that because You died for all, we who live should no longer live for ourselves but for You who died for us and was raised again (2 Cor. 5:14–15).

MOST OF US WOULD NEVER ACKNOWLEDGE GOD AS GOD ALONE IF WE DIDN'T EXPERIENCE CRISES WHEN NO ONE ELSE COULD HELP.

Lord God, if I feel hated by the world, You have told me to keep in mind that it hated You first. You said that if I belonged to the world, it would love me as its own.

As it is, I do not belong to the world, but You, awesome and magnificent God, have chosen me out of the world. That is why the world hates me.

Help me to remember the words You spoke to me: "No servant is greater than his master." If they persecuted You, they will persecute me also. If they obeyed Your teaching, they will obey the teaching of Your disciples also (John 15:18–20).

Even if my father and mother forsake me, You, Lord, will receive me (Ps. 27:10).

WE CAN EASILY BE LED INTO CAPTIVITY BY SEEKING OTHER ANSWERS TO NEEDS AND DESIRES THAT ONLY GOD CAN MEET.

O God, I desperately need Your discernment when something may be permissible for me but not necessarily beneficial. Please empower me to resist things that are not beneficial for me so that I will not be mastered by anything! (1 Cor. 6:12).

Help me to truly embrace the fact that my body is a temple of the Holy Spirit, who is in me, whom I have received from God. I am not my own (1 Cor. 6:19). Thank You, Father! I am so much better off belonging to You than belonging to myself!

You found my life worth buying at a tremendously high price. Therefore please help me honor You with my body (1 Cor. 6:20).

THE WORLD SEES CHRISTIANS AS PEOPLE WHO USE FAITH AS A CRUTCH. HOW WRONG THEY ARE. THE BIGGEST CRUTCH OF ALL IS DECEIT.

Lord God, help me not to allow the worries of this life, the deceitfulness of wealth, and the desires for other things to come in and choke Your Word, making it unfruitful in my life (Mark 4:19).

According to Your Word, if physical things were allowed to completely satisfy us, our hearts would become proud, and we would forget the Lord our God, who brought us out of the land of slavery (Deut. 8:12–14).

I have been crucified with You, Christ, and I no longer live, but You live in me. The life I live in the body, I live by faith in You, the Son of God, who loved me and gave Yourself for me (Gal. 2:20).

You are not defined by anything that happened to you or anything you've done. you are defined by who you are in christ.

Lord, I have no reason to be ashamed, because I know whom I have believed, and am convinced that You are able to guard what I have entrusted to You for that day (2 Tim. 1:12). Even when I've been faithless, You've been faithful, for You cannot disown Yourself (2 Tim. 2:13).

Help me not to fall victim to the accusations of Satan, the accuser of believers. He is furious because he knows his time is short. I have received Your salvation and I am in Your kingdom, under the authority of Your Son, Jesus Christ. The enemy is overcome by the blood of the Lamb and by the word of our testimonies (Rev. 12:10–11). Help me never cease testifying of Your mighty work in me.

JUNE

GOD HEARS THE WORDS AND COMMUNICATIONS OF OUR MINDS AS CLEARLY AS HUMAN EARS HEAR OUR SPOKEN WORDS.

Help me trust in You at all times; help me to pour out my heart to You, God, for You are my refuge (Ps. 62:8).

O Lord, help me not be afraid to speak to You what's on my heart. Your Word says You know my thoughts and my actions, and You know what I'm going to say before a word forms on my tongue (Ps. 139:1–4).

You will never be offended when I pour out the earnest despair and bitterness that wells in my heart. You desire for me to cry out in my agony, and You can take my feelings of anger, dismay, and confusion.

In pouring my heart out to You, I rid myself of soul-cancerous bitterness. I also make room for You to pour in Your healing.

THE BIGGEST SACRIFICES OF OUR
LIVES WILL BE THOSE TIMES WHEN WE
CHOSE OUR OWN WAY AND FORFEITED
GOD'S PLEASING WILL FOR US.

Your ways are not my ways, Lord God. As the heavens are higher than the earth, so are Your ways higher than mine (Isa. 55:8–9). I may not always understand Your ways, Lord, but they are always prosperous (Ps. 10:5). Your ways are always righteous (Ps. 145:17). Your ways, O God, are holy (Ps. 77:13). Your ways are loving and faithful (Ps. 25:10).

I have considered my ways, Lord (Ps. 119:59). I choose Yours instead. Keep me from deceitful ways (Ps. 119:29). Lord God, help me to walk in Your ways (Ps. 119:3).

Lord, if being obedient to You causes me to suffer, I know I should commit myself to my faithful Creator and continue to do good (1 Pet. 4:19).

WE READILY ACCEPT GOD'S LOVE FOR OTHERS BUT STRUGGLE WITH THE BELIEF THAT HE LOVES US EQUALLY, RADICALLY, COMPLETELY.

Blessed am I, Lord, because You are faithful to correct me. I will not despise the discipline of the Almighty.

I have despised my life at times. I have wanted people to leave me alone because I've felt my days had no meaning (Job 5:17; 7:16). Lord, You would not leave me here on this earth a single day that was not meant to have meaning. My life does have meaning. Please help me not to despise it or isolate others from it.

Lord God, help me to be obedient to You even in this difficult season. Your Word says that even in darkness light dawns for the upright, for the gracious and compassionate and righteous man (Ps. 112:4).

I FIND GREAT COMFORT IN KNOWING
CHRIST DOESN'T THROW HIS HAND
OVER HIS MOUTH IN SHOCK WHEN I
WISH I COULD ACT A CERTAIN WAY.

Lord God, since I have a great high priest who has gone through the heavens, Jesus Your Son, help me hold firmly to the faith I profess. For I do not have a high priest who is unable to sympathize with my weaknesses, but I have one who has been tempted in every way, just as I am, yet was without sin.

Help me then to approach the throne of grace with confidence, so that I may receive mercy and find grace to help me in my time of need (Heb. 4:14–16).

Help me draw near to You, God, with a sincere heart in full assurance of faith, having my heart sprinkled to cleanse me from a guilty conscience and having my body washed with pure water (Heb. 10:22).

Rebellion can begin with fun and games, but eventually it leads to hard work. God allows it to become a heavy burden.

Do not withhold Your mercy from me, O Lord; may Your love and Your truth always protect me. For troubles without number surround me; my sins have overtaken me, and I cannot see. They are more than the hairs of my head, and my heart fails within me. Be pleased, O Lord, to save me; O Lord, come quickly to help me (Ps. 40:11–13).

From the ends of the earth I call to You, O Lord. I call as my heart grows faint; lead me to the rock that is higher than I. For You have been my refuge, a strong tower against the foe (Ps. 61:2–3). O Lord, be my rock of refuge, to which I can always go; give the command to save me, for You are my rock and my fortress (Ps. 71:3).

LONG BEFORE THE FIRST BILLION DOLLARS WAS INVESTED IN EXPLORING SPACE, GOD'S OWN HANDS STRETCHED THE HEAVENS.

Since the creation of the world Your invisible qualities—Your eternal power and divine nature—have been clearly seen, being understood from what has been made, so that men are without excuse (Rom. 1:20). Help us not exchange the truth of God for a lie, and worship and serve created things rather than You, our Creator—who is forever praised. Amen! (Rom. 1:25).

This is what You, the Lord my God, say—You who created the heavens, You are God; You who fashioned and made the earth, You founded it; You did not create it to be empty, but formed it to be inhabited—You say: "I am the Lord, and there is no other" (Isa. 45:18).

I NOT ONLY LOVE GOD AND TRUST
HIM, I LOVE TRUSTING HIM. IT IS
A CONSTANT REMINDER OF A
PERPETUAL MIRACLE IN MY LIFE.

Lord, just as Your apostles pled and ultimately received, I ask you also to increase my
faith! (Luke 17:5).

Father, I want You to be able to look at my
life as You did Stephen's and be able to say that
I am full of the Holy Spirit and faith, and that
many people were brought to the Lord through
my witness (Acts 11:24).

Just as You did through Paul and Barnabas
to the early disciples, strengthen this disciple
and encourage me to remain true to the faith,
for Your Word says, "We must go through
many hardships to enter the kingdom of God"
(Acts 14:22).

Thank You, God, for purifying my heart
by faith (Acts 15:9).

FEW THINGS ARE MORE CONTRARY TO OUR HUMAN NATURES THAN DESIRING ANYONE'S FAME ABOVE OUR OWN.

Father, according to Your Word, the fear of the Lord teaches a man wisdom, and humility comes before honor (Prov. 15:33). Again, Your Word says, "Before his downfall a man's heart is proud, but humility comes before honor" (Prov. 18:12). I want to be a person of honor in Your sight, O, God. This goal is possible only with humility. Help me to have a humble disposition.

Father, help me possess only acceptable kinds of pride such as taking pride in those who set a good example and those who encourage others by their faithful walk with You. (2 Cor. 5:12). Then, even in all our troubles, as we take godly pride in one another, our joy may know no bounds (2 Cor. 7:4).

THE PRIMARY REASON GOD'S WORD CAN HAVE SUCH AN EFFECT ON A BELIEVER'S LIFE IS ITS VITAL ASSOCIATION WITH THE HOLY SPIRIT.

Father, You sent Your Holy Spirit to be a Counselor to me. He came straight from You to me and other believers. He is the Spirit of truth who goes out from the Father, and He faithfully testifies truth to me concerning Your Son, Jesus (John 15:26).

Lord God, sanctify me by the truth; Your Word is truth (John 17:17). Please help me to embrace fully what this verse is saying, Lord. I can be saved by You, but if I don't allow You to teach me and mature me through Your Word, I will never fulfill what You sanctified or set me apart in this earthly existence to do.

Father God, You have no greater joy than to hear that Your children are walking in the truth (3 John 4).

WHEN WE OFFER A TRUSTING HEART AND AN HONEST, OPEN MIND TO GOD, RENEWAL IS ON ITS WAY.

Father God, according to Your Word, the angel of the Lord encamps around those who fear You, and You deliver them. Continually whet my appetite and woo me to taste and see that You are good; blessed am I when I take refuge in You!

Lord God, please continue to develop in me the right kind of fear of You, because Your Word says that those who fear You lack nothing. The lions may grow weak and hungry, but those who seek You, Lord, lack no good thing (Ps. 34:7–10).

Thank You, Lord, for always being good, a refuge in times of trouble. You care for those who trust in You (Nah. 1:7).

JESUS FLAUNTS HIS LOVE FOR YOU. HE WAVES HIS HAND OVER YOU, SIGNALING TO ALL IN SIGHT THAT YOU ARE THE ONE HE LOVES.

Lord Jesus, as unimaginable as this may seem, when I am obedient to You, You call me friend. You desire to make known to me everything You learned from Your Father!

I did not choose You, Lord, but You chose me and appointed me to go and bear fruit—fruit that will last. Then the Father will give me whatever I ask in Your name (John 15:13–16).

Develop Your heart within me, Jesus, so I will know how to ask of the Father in Your great name. Help me also to be perpetually aware that You chose me, so I never need to feel left out. You have loved me and known me from the foundation of the world.

YOU WERE NEVER MEANT TO GO
THROUGH LIFE BY THE SKIN OF YOUR
TEETH BUT TO FLOURISH IN THE LOVE
AND ACCEPTANCE OF ALMIGHTY GOD.

No matter what I once was, I have been
washed, I have been sanctified, and I have been
justified in the name of the Lord Jesus Christ
and by the Spirit of our God! (I Cor. 6:11).

Father, Your Word says that when the time
had fully come, You sent Your Son, born of a
woman, born under law, to redeem those under law, that we might receive the full rights of
sons. Because I am a son, You sent the Spirit of
Your Son into my heart, the Spirit who calls
out, "Abba, Father" (Gal. 4:4–6). I am Your
child! I have the full right of a son! And it is my
right to be free in You!

I celebrate as fact that I am no longer a
slave, but a child; and since I am a child, You
have made me also an heir (Gal. 4:7).

THE ONE WHO ADOPTED US INTO
HIS ROYAL FAMILY HAS CALLED US TO
LIVE ACCORDING TO OUR LEGACY.
WE ARE LITERALLY TO LIVE LOVE.

I am among Your chosen people, O Lord, Your royal priesthood, Your holy nation. I am part of a people belonging to You, that I may openly declare Your praises, the One who called me out of darkness into Your wonderful light (1 Pet. 2:9).

Dear God, as one of Your own, please help me to flee from sin and pursue righteousness, godliness, faith, love, endurance, and gentleness (1 Tim. 6:11).

Above all else, help me to love You with all my heart and with all my soul and with all my strength (Deut. 6:5). Help me to live a life of love, just as Christ loved me and gave Himself up for me as a fragrant offering and sacrifice to You (Eph. 5:2).

AS WE RETURN TO GOD AND REST CONFIDENTLY IN HIS PROMISES AND POWER, WE CONTINUALLY FIND SALVATION.

Father, my guilt overwhelms me at times like a burden too heavy to bear. . . . I am bowed down and brought very low; all day long I go about mourning. . . . I am feeble and utterly crushed; I groan in anguish of heart.

All my longings lie open before You, O Lord; my sighing is not hidden from You. My heart pounds, my strength fails me; even the light has gone from my eyes. . . . I confess my iniquity; I am troubled by my sin.

O Lord, do not forsake me; be not far from me, O my God. Come quickly to help me, O Lord my Savior (Ps. 38:4, 6, 8–10, 18, 21–22). Father, You never reject the truly repentant. Thank You, Lord.

COMMIT YOURSELF ENTIRELY TO GOD THAT HE MAY SET YOU FREE TO BE EVERYTHING HE PLANNED.

I want to trust in You with all my heart and lean not on my own understanding; in all my ways I will acknowledge You, and You will make my paths straight (Prov. 3:5–6). For You know the plans You have for me, Lord. Plans to prosper me and not to harm me, plans to give me a hope and a future (Jer. 29:11).

I desire to dwell in the shelter of You, the Most High. I will rest in the shadow of the Almighty. I will say of You, Lord, "You are my refuge and my fortress, my God, in whom I trust" (Ps. 91:1–2).

Faithful Lord, because You are my help, I sing in the shadow of Your wings. My soul clings to You, and Your right hand upholds me (Ps. 63:7–8).

FORGIVENESS MEANS DEFERRING THE CAUSE TO CHRIST AND DECIDING TO BE FREE OF THE ONGOING BURDEN OF BITTERNESS AND BLAME.

O Lord, You will take up my case; You will redeem my life. You have seen the wrong done to me. Uphold my cause! (Lam. 3:58–59).

Lord, help me to see that when You are upholding my cause, I don't have to. Help me to lay this burden down and let You carry it instead.

O Lord, I desire not to grieve the Holy Spirit of God, with whom I was sealed for the day of redemption. By the power of Your Spirit, help me to get rid of all bitterness, rage and anger, brawling and slander, along with every form of malice. I desire to be kind and compassionate to others, forgiving others, just as in Christ You forgave me (Eph. 4:30–32).

Satan will do anything he can to scare you away from your God-ordained destiny.

Lord God, the cords of death have entangled Your child, the anguish of the grave has come upon me; I have been overcome by trouble and sorrow. . . . But now, O Lord, You will deliver my soul from death, my eyes from tears, my feet from stumbling (Ps. 116:3, 8).

The thief comes only to steal and kill and destroy; But You, Lord Jesus, have come that I may have life, and have it to the full (John 10:10).

I acknowledge, O my God, that Your will for me is abundant life. Full life! Satan, the thief, has come to steal, kill, and destroy all things concerning my life. I stand against him in Your name and desire to accept the abundant life You came to bring me.

ALL OUR LIVES GOD RETAINS THE STRONG FEELINGS TOWARD US THAT INFANTS EVOKE IN THEIR PARENTS. HE NEVER HAS TO LET US GO.

O Lord, You have searched me and You know me. You know when I sit and when I rise; You perceive my thoughts from afar. You discern my going out and my lying down; You are familiar with all my ways (Ps. 139:1–3).

Father, I thank You that while You love me completely, You know everything about me. Help me to be completely truthful with You. I don't need to hide anymore.

Lord God, if I claim to be without sin, I deceive myself and the truth is not in me. If I confess my sins, You are faithful and just and will forgive my sins and purify me from all unrighteousness (1 John 1:9). Father, please help me to accept the fact that I have not outsinned Your ability to forgive me!

IF OUR HEARTS ARE HUMBLE AND
RIGHT BEFORE GOD, WE CAN HAND
OVER TO HIM ALL THE CONFLICTS
AND FOES THAT RISE UP AGAINST US.

Lord, my God, show the wonder of Your great love, You who save by Your right hand those who take refuge in You from their foes. Keep me as the apple of Your eye; hide me in the shadow of Your wings from the wicked who assail me (Ps. 17:7–9).

Reach down from on high, my God and my Redeemer, and take hold of me! Draw me out of deep waters. Rescue me from my powerful enemy, from my foes, who are too strong for me!

My enemy has confronted me in the day of my disaster, but You, Lord, are my support! Bring me to a spacious place; rescue me because You delight in me! (Ps. 18:16–19).

Victorious lives flow from victorious thoughts, from setting our focus on a victorious God.

You, my Christ, are the image of the invisible God, the firstborn over all creation. For by You all things were created: things in heaven and on earth, visible and invisible, whether thrones or powers or rulers or authorities; all things were created by You and for You. You are before all things, and in You all things hold together (Col. 1:15–17).

Where can I go from Your Spirit? Where can I flee from Your presence? If I go up to the heavens, You are there; if I make my bed in the depths, You are there. If I rise on the wings of the dawn, if I settle on the far side of the sea, even there Your hand will guide me, Your right hand will hold me fast (Ps. 139:7–10).

GOD DELIGHTS IN YOUR ATTENTIONS EVEN WHEN YOU PRACTICE THEM MUCH LIKE YOU DID YESTERDAY.

Christ Jesus, You said, "The work of God is this: to believe the one he has sent" (John 6:29). That is what You want from me more than anything in the world.

You said that those who believe You are Your sheep. Your sheep listen to Your voice; You know them, and they follow You. You give them eternal life, and they shall never perish; no one can snatch them out of Your Father's hand. You and the Father are one (John 10:26–30).

Father, how I thank You that I am not of those who shrink back and are destroyed but of those who believe and are saved (Heb. 10:39).

WE ARE NEVER A MORE BEAUTIFUL DISPLAY OF GOD'S SPLENDOR THAN WHEN WILLING TO EMPTY SELF FOR THE LIVES OF OTHERS.

Father, You have told me to do nothing out of selfish ambition or vain conceit but in humility to consider others better than myself (Phil. 2:3). Right this moment, I confess all selfish ambition and vain conceit to You. Forgive me for so often considering myself better than others. Help me to look not only to my own interests but also to the interests of others. Please give me an attitude the same as that of Christ Jesus (Phil. 2:4–5).

Father, help me to clothe myself with humility toward others, because You oppose the proud but give grace to the humble (1 Pet. 5:5). I will never live a day that I am not in need of Your grace, so please help me maintain an attitude that welcomes it.

We're all looking for a quick fix, but God is after lasting change. He leads us to a lifestyle of Christianity.

Lord, I desire to become mature, attaining to the whole measure of the fullness of Christ. Then I will no longer be an infant, tossed back and forth by the waves, and blown here and there by every wind of teaching and by the cunning and craftiness of men in their deceitful scheming. Instead, teach me to speak the truth in love, growing up into Him who is the head, that is, Christ (Eph. 4:13–15).

Enable me to stand firm, with the belt of truth buckled around my waist and with the breastplate of righteousness in place (Eph. 6:14). Help me to understand that without the girding of truth, I am defenseless against the devil. Truth is my main defense against the father of lies.

EVERY HUMAN BEING LONGS FOR
UNFAILING LOVE. LAVISH LOVE.
FOCUSED LOVE. RADICAL LOVE.
LOVE WE CAN COUNT ON.

Lord, I believe that Your feelings toward me are consistent with Your feelings toward Your people, Israel, for You are the same yesterday, today, and forever. Therefore I believe You bless the praying of Your words to Israel as words over my own life too.

This is what You say—You who created me, who formed me: "Fear not, for I have redeemed you; I have summoned you by name; you are mine. When you pass through the waters, I will be with you; and when you pass through the rivers, they will not sweep over you. When you walk through the fire, you will not be burned; the flames will not set you ablaze. For I am the Lord, your God, the Holy One of Israel, your Savior" (Isa. 43:1–4).

The only thing we absolutely could not survive would be the loss of God's love. And that is a loss we'll never have to try.

You, Lord, are my shepherd; I shall not be in want. You make me lie down in green pastures; You lead me beside quiet waters; You restore my soul. You guide me in paths of righteousness for Your name's sake.

Even though I walk through the valley of the shadow of death, I will fear no evil, for You are with me; Your rod and Your staff, they comfort me.

You prepare a table before me in the presence of my enemies. You anoint my head with oil; my cup overflows.

Surely goodness and love will follow me all the days of my life, and I will dwell in the house of the Lord forever (Ps. 23:1–6).

TO EXPERIENCE FREEDOM AND VICTORY, WE NEED TO BECOME CAPTIVES. WE NEED TO DEVELOP MINDS CAPTIVE TO CHRIST.

Lord, because I have accepted Christ as my Savior, Your Word says that I am controlled not by the sinful nature but by the Spirit, because the Spirit of God lives in me. And if anyone does not have the Spirit of Christ, he does not belong to Christ (Rom. 8:9).

Father, according to Your Word, since Christ is in me, my body is dead because of sin, yet my spirit is alive because of righteousness (Rom. 8:10). And if the Spirit of Him who raised Jesus from the dead is living in me, He who raised Christ from the dead will also give life to my mortal body through His Spirit, who lives in me! (Rom. 8:11).

WALKING CONSISTENTLY DOES NOT MEAN WALKING PERFECTLY. IT MEANS WE MAY STUMBLE, BUT WE WILL NOT FALL.

According to Your Word, it is better not to make a vow than to make a vow and not fulfill it (Eccles. 5:5). Please help me to realize that the power to be victorious does not come from my ability to make and keep a vow out of pure determination. Sooner or later, I will fail if I'm only trying to fulfill a vow.

The power to be victorious comes from realizing the vow You have already made to me when You gave me Your Spirit and Your Word. As Your Word says in Zechariah 4:6, success won't come by might nor by power, but by the Spirit of the Lord Almighty!

Therefore, what You are commanding me today is not too difficult for me or beyond my reach (Deut. 30:11). You will strengthen me!

HE IS FAITHFUL TO CHASTISE, OR HOW WOULD WE LEARN FROM OUR REBELLION? BUT HE IS ALSO COMPASSIONATE IN HIS COMFORT.

Father God, thank You for having no condemnation for those who are in Christ Jesus, because through Christ Jesus the law of the Spirit of life set me free from the law of sin and death.

For what the law was powerless to do in that it was weakened by the sinful nature, You did by sending Your own Son in the likeness of sinful man to be a sin offering (Rom. 8:1–3).

Therefore, help me to understand, Lord, that the loving chastisement that might come to me after I have rebelled against You is only in the Father's purest love and is never to be confused with condemnation (Heb. 12:6).

Have you sometimes experienced defeat because you refused to calm yourself in the presence of God and trust him?

God, You are my refuge and strength, an ever-present help in trouble. Therefore I will not fear, though the earth give way and the mountains fall into the heart of the sea, though its waters roar and foam and the mountains quake with their surging.

I will be still and know You are God. You, Lord Almighty, are with me. You, God of Jacob, are my fortress (Ps. 46:1–2, 10–11). A father to the fatherless, a defender of widows, are You in Your holy dwelling (Ps. 68:5).

I commit my way to You, Lord; I trust in You and You will do this: You will make my righteousness shine like the dawn, the justice of my cause like the noonday sun (Ps. 37:5–6).

YOU MIGHT BE RELIEVED TO KNOW THAT WE CAN LOVE WITHOUT FEELING ALL WARM AND FUZZY. WE LIVE BY FAITH. WE LOVE BY FAITH.

Lord Jesus, Your precious blood of the covenant was poured out for many for the forgiveness of sins (Matt. 26:28). After You poured out Your own blood for my forgiveness, help me not respond with a heart too hard to forgive others.

According to Your Word, love is the most excellent way to deal with anything (I Cor. 12:31). So please help me to live in harmony with others and be sympathetic toward others, loving as a sister or a brother, being compassionate and humble. Help me never to repay evil with evil or insult with insult, but with blessing, because to this I was called so that I may inherit a blessing (I Pet. 3:8–9).

JULY

SATAN HAS NO RIGHT TO EXERCISE AUTHORITY OVER US, BUT HE HOPES WE'RE TOO IGNORANT REGARDING SCRIPTURE TO KNOW IT.

Lord, Your Word asks, "Who among you fears the Lord and obeys the word of his servant?" Your Word then exhorts, "Let him who walks in the dark, who has no light, trust in the name of the Lord and rely on his God" (Isa. 50:10). Father, I desire to trust in the name of my Lord and rely on You, my God, even when walking through dark times.

My struggle is not against flesh and blood but against the rulers, against the authorities, against the powers of this dark world, and against the spiritual forces of evil in the heavenly realms (Eph. 6:12). I must not be naïve and deny how much Satan desires to take control of this season of my life. Help me to stand firm against attacks!

IF YOU ARE STRIVING DAILY TO GIVE
GOD YOUR HEART AND MIND AND ARE
SENSITIVE TO SIN IN YOUR THOUGHT
LIFE, I'D CALL YOU GODLY.

Lord God, Your Word says that You bless the home of the righteous but Your curse is on the house of the wicked (Prov. 3:33). Lord, please help me cleanse my home of any kind of materials that support or fuel wickedness. Make this the kind of home You can fully bless.

Lord, You detest perversity, but You take the upright into Your confidence (Prov. 3:32). Please make me a person You can take into Your confidence.

Lord God, help me to guard my heart above all else, for it is the wellspring of life. Help me to put away perversity from my mouth and keep corrupt talk far from my lips (Prov. 4:23–24).

GOD IS NOT ONLY THE ANSWER TO A
THOUSAND NEEDS BUT A THOUSAND
WANTS. HE IS THE FULFILLMENT OF
OUR CHIEF DESIRE IN ALL OF LIFE.

O Lord, let the morning bring me word of Your unfailing love, for I have put my trust in You. Show me the way I should go, for to You I lift up my soul.

Rescue me from my enemies, Lord, for I hide myself in You. Teach me to do Your will, for You are my God; may Your good Spirit lead me on level ground.

For Your name's sake, O Lord, preserve my life; in Your righteousness, bring me out of trouble. In Your unfailing love, silence my enemies; destroy all my foes, for I am Your servant (Ps. 143:8–12). I trust in You, Lord, to rescue me. Teach me to delight in You, and deliver me, O God (Ps. 22:8).

HE IS OUR LIFE'S PROTECTION,
BUT ALSO OUR HEART'S AFFECTION.
HE IS OUR SOUL'S SALVATION, BUT
ALSO OUR HEART'S EXHILARATION.

Your love, O Lord, reaches to the heavens, Your faithfulness to the skies. Your righteousness is like the mighty mountains, Your justice like the great deep. O Lord, You preserve both man and beast. How priceless is Your unfailing love!

Both high and low among men find refuge in the shadow of Your wings. I want to feast on the abundance of Your house; I want to drink from Your river of delights. For with You is the fountain of life; in Your light I want to see light (Ps. 36:5–9).

You are the Lord; that is Your name! You will not give Your glory to another or Your praise to idols (Isa. 42:8). You, my Lord, are a warrior; the Lord is Your name (Exod. 15:3).

SATAN WANTS TO DESTROY OUR
DREAMS. GOD WANTS TO SURPASS
THEM. HE GIVES US DREAMS SO
WE'LL LONG FOR HIS REALITY.

Father, Your Word is full of fulfilled
prophecy. You told things before they happened so that when they did, people would
believe (John 14:29). And as surely as everything You prophesied in the past has happened,
everything You prophesied for the future will
happen. Help me to believe!

I ask You to help me to receive the Word
of God not as the word of men but as it actually is, the Word of God, which is at work in
me as one who believes (1 Thess. 2:13).

Through Christ I believe in You who
raised Him from the dead and glorified Him.
My faith and hope are in You! (1 Pet. 1:21).

God didn't promise the children of israel a place they could visit. he promised them a place they could settle and dwell in.

Father, in Your Word, You define who is wise and understanding: the one who shows it by his good life, by deeds done in the humility that comes from wisdom (James 3:13).

But Father, it is not enough for me to humble myself for one day (Isa. 58:5). You desire humility to be a lifestyle characteristic.

Like the apostle Paul, help me to serve You, Lord, with great humility and with tears, even when I am severely tested (Acts 20:19). Like Mary, help my soul to glorify You and my spirit rejoice in You my Savior, for You have been mindful of the humble state of Your servant (Luke 1:46–48).

WHEN WE RESPOND TO ATTACKS OF
DOUBT, DISTORTION, AND DECEIT
WITH THE TRUTH OF GOD'S WORD,
THE FIERY DART IS EXTINGUISHED.

God, according to Your Word, people perish because they refuse to love the truth and so be saved (2 Thess. 2:10). Please, Lord, give me a love for truth! Immeasurable fruit is produced by the love of truth.

Lord, Your Word is clear that those who are self-seeking, who reject the truth, and who continue following evil will experience Your wrath and anger (Rom. 2:8).

Father God, in all sincerity, I desire to renounce all secret and shameful ways; I want to forsake the use of all deception, and learn not to distort the Word of God. On the contrary, by setting forth the truth plainly, I desire to commend myself to every man's conscience in the sight of God (2 Cor. 4:2).

WHATEVER THE CAUSE OF OUR
MOURNING, CHRIST CAN BE THE
LIFTER OF OUR HEADS. HE CAN GIVE
US BEAUTY INSTEAD OF ASHES.

Help me to call this to mind and therefore always have hope: because of Your great love, I am not consumed, for Your compassions never fail. They are new toward me every morning; great is Your faithfulness. I will say to myself, "The Lord is my portion; therefore I will wait for Him" (Lam. 3:22–24).

I will be glad and rejoice in Your love, O God, for You saw my affliction and knew the anguish of my soul. You have not handed me over to the enemy but have set my feet in a spacious place (Ps. 31:7–8). Hallelujah!

You, eternal God, are my refuge, and underneath are Your everlasting arms. You will drive out my enemy before me, saying, "Destroy him!" (Deut. 33:27).

HE FLOODS ONLY THE PARTS OF OUR
LIVES WHERE HE IS IN AUTHORITY.
FREEDOM FLOWS WHERE THE SPIRIT
OF THE LORD FLOODS.

Lord Jesus, You said that if anyone loves You, he will obey Your teaching. You also assured that Your Father would love him and that both of You would come to him and make Your home with him (John 14:23). O Lord, I pray that You would dwell in me richly and fully through Your Holy Spirit. Make my heart Your home, Lord Jesus.

You will not take Your love from me. You will never betray Your own faithfulness. You will not violate Your covenant or alter what Your lips have uttered (Ps. 89:33–34).

My faithful God who is the same yesterday, today, and forever (Heb. 13:8), be to me what You were to Abram: my shield and my very great reward (Gen. 15:1).

OUR GLORIOUS INHERITANCE IN
CHRIST IS NOT MEANT FOR HEAVEN
ALONE. IT SHOULD ALSO HAVE AN
IMPACT ON OUR EARTHLY EXISTENCE.

Father and God of our Lord Jesus Christ,
please give me the Spirit of wisdom and revelation, so that I may know You better. I pray also
that the eyes of my heart may be enlightened
in order that I may know the hope to which
You have called me, the riches of Your glorious
inheritance in the saints (Eph. 1:17–18).

Father, Your incomparably great power is
available for us who believe. This power is like
the working of Your mighty strength, which
You exerted in Christ when You raised Him
from the dead and seated Him at Your right
hand in the heavenly realms (Eph. 1:19–20). If
You can raise Jesus from the dead and seat Him
beside You, You can deliver me!

CHRIST STILL GRIEVES WHEN HE SEES
HEARTS IN UNNECESSARY TURMOIL.
BUT WE MUST BELIEVE, BEND THE
KNEE, AND RECEIVE HIS PEACE.

Lord God, according to Your Word, everyone born of You overcomes the world. This is the victory that has overcome the world, even our faith. Who is it that overcomes the world? I do, when I truly believe that Jesus is the Son of God (1 John 5:4–5).

Christ Jesus, You Yourself are my peace, who has . . . destroyed the barrier, the dividing wall of hostility, by abolishing in Your flesh the law with its commandments and regulations (Eph. 2:14–15).

Continue to teach me with regard to my former way of life, to put off my old self . . . and to put on the new self, created to be like You, God, in true righteousness and holiness (Eph. 4:22–24).

All that time I thought God was counting my sins, and he was counting my faith as righteousness instead.

Wash me, Lord, and I will be whiter than snow. Let me hear joy and gladness; let the bones You have crushed rejoice! (Ps. 51:7–8). Break this bondage, Lord, that seems to keep me from sensing or believing Your forgiveness. Help me to rejoice that the only thing whiter than snow is a repentant sinner!

Blessed am I, God, because my transgressions are forgiven. My sins are covered. Blessed am I because You, Lord, will never count my sins against me (Rom. 4:7–8).

O, how I praise You that everyone who believes in You, Jesus, receives forgiveness of sins through Your name! (Acts 10:43). There are no exceptions!

If satan has convinced you to see yourself as anything less than a handpicked child of God, Christ can restore your lost dignity.

Help me, Lord God, to know beyond a shadow of a doubt that in all things You work for the good of those who love You, those who have been called according to Your purpose (Rom. 8:28).

Please help me to see the condition in that promise. You are not obligated to work all things together for good for those who neither love You nor are called according to Your purpose. You obligate Yourself to this awesome promise when I offer You my aching heart and commit myself and my suffering to Your good purposes.

If I do, You will do more with my life than I could ever conceive (1 Cor. 2:9).

I WOULD NEVER IMPLY THAT
GETTING OVER REJECTION IS EASY,
BUT IT IS GOD'S UNQUESTIONABLE
WILL FOR YOUR LIFE.

Lord, help me to obey You and not repay anyone evil for evil. Help me to be careful to do what is right in the eyes of everybody. If it is possible, as far as it depends on me, I want to live at peace with everyone.

Help me not to take revenge but leave room for Your wrath, for You have written: "It is mine to avenge; I will repay." On the contrary: if my enemy is hungry, help me to feed him; if he is thirsty, help me to give him something to drink. In doing this, I will heap burning coals on his head (Rom. 12:17–20).

O Father, please cause the love of Christ to compel me to do what is right in this challenging situation (2 Cor. 5:14).

A POWERFUL MOTIVATION FOR
BELIEVING GOD IN OUR PRESENT IS
INTENTIONALLY REMEMBERING HOW
HE'S WORKED IN OUR PAST.

Lord, if the only home I hope for is the grave, if I spread out my bed in darkness . . . where then is my hope? (Job 17:13, 15). Help me not to see the grave as my only hope. I am one of Your children, Lord! How foolish for the grave to be my hope, for I will never live in a grave. I will be with You in glory.

For You who said, "Let light shine out of darkness," made Your light shine in my heart to give me the light of the knowledge of the glory of God in the face of Christ (2 Cor. 4:6). I am a chosen person, part of a royal priesthood, a holy nation, a people belonging to You, God, that I may declare the praises of You who called me out of darkness into Your wonderful light (1 Pet. 2:9).

UNTIL WE CHOOSE TO WITHHOLD NO PART OF OUR LIVES FROM HIS AUTHORITY, WE WILL NOT EXPERIENCE FULL FREEDOM.

Lord God, I know that the wicked will not inherit the kingdom of God. I choose to be deceived no longer: neither the sexually immoral nor idolaters nor adulterers nor male prostitutes nor homosexual offenders nor thieves nor the greedy nor drunkards nor slanderers nor swindlers will inherit the kingdom of God. And I have been some of those things.

But I have now been washed. I have been sanctified, I have been justified in the name of the Lord Jesus Christ and by the Spirit of my God (1 Cor. 6:9–11). Lord God, guard my course and protect my way as I pursue a righteous, victorious life in You (Prov. 2:8).

WE CAN BE LED ASTRAY BY THE CORDS OF AN EVIL YOKE, OR WE CAN BE LED TO VICTORY BY THE CORDS OF DIVINE LOVE.

Who is my God, except for You, Lord? And who is my Rock except for my God?

It is You, God, who arms me with strength and makes my way perfect. You make my feet like the feet of a deer; You enable me to stand on the heights. You train my hands for battle (Ps. 18:31–34).

You give me Your shield of victory; Your right hand sustains me; You stoop down to make me great. You broaden the path beneath me, so that my ankles do not turn. . . . Arm me with strength for the battle; make my adversary bow at my feet. Make my enemy turn back in flight. Thank You, God! One day You will utterly destroy my foe! (Ps. 18:35–36, 39–40).

I BELIEVE THAT THE GREATEST
MIRACLE OF ALL IS WHEN GLORY
COMES TO THE FATHER THROUGH
MORTAL CREATURES LIKE US.

Great are You, my Lord, and most worthy
of praise. Your greatness no one can fathom.

One generation will commend Your works
to another; they will tell of Your mighty acts.
They will speak of the glorious splendor of
Your majesty, and I will meditate on Your wonderful works. They will tell of the power of
Your awesome works, and I will proclaim Your
great deeds. They will celebrate Your abundant
goodness and joyfully sing of Your righteousness (Ps. 145:3–7).

You, my God, are the Rock. Your works
are perfect, and all Your ways are just. You are a
faithful God who does no wrong. You are upright and just (Deut. 32:4).

Don't confess your sin by telling god how you're going to do better. just run to the father and rest in him.

Lord God, I know that it was not with perishable things such as silver or gold that I was redeemed from the empty way of life handed down to me from my forefathers but with the precious blood of Christ, a lamb without blemish or defect. He was chosen before the creation of the world but was revealed in these last times for my sake. Through Him I believe in God, who raised Him from the dead and glorified Him, and so my faith and hope are in God (I Pet. 1:18–21).

Father, thank You for helping me to understand that the access I have gained into Your grace in which I now stand has come to me by faith. Help me to rejoice in the hope of Your glory! (Rom. 5:2).

IF WE WISH TO GO FORWARD FROM
HERE, GOD MUST EMPOWER US TO
ROLL THE BOULDER OF PRIDE OFF
OUR ROAD TO LIBERTY.

Father, You are calling upon me to be completely humble and gentle; to be patient, bearing with others in love (Eph. 4:2). Please empower me with Your Spirit to be obedient to this command.

You've warned me that when pride comes, then comes disgrace, but with humility comes wisdom (Prov. 11:2). You instruct Your people to listen carefully and heed Your instruction because pride can cause the Lord's flock to be taken captive (Jer. 13:17).

But You promise to guide the humble in what is right and teach them Your way (Ps. 25:9). Give me a humble heart so I will follow You in what is right and learn Your way.

FRIVOLOUS ARGUMENTS CAN DILUTE
SPIRITUAL TRUTHS INTO HUMAN
LOGIC. WE ARE NOT CALLED TO
DEBATE FAITH BUT TO DO IT.

Lord, without You I would be foolish, disobedient, deceived, and enslaved by all kinds of passions and pleasures. I would live in ongoing malice and envy, being hated and hating others (Titus 3:3).

I don't want that kind of life, God! I want to live life in the power and fullness of Your Spirit. Lord, I want You to have the great joy of hearing others talk about my faithfulness to the truth and how I continue to walk in the truth (3 John 3).

You have adamantly warned Your children not to be deceived (James 1:16). Am I presently being deceived in any way? If I am, please reveal it to me and give me the courage to cease cooperating with deceptive schemes.

WAIT ON HIM TO BRING VICTORY,
KNOWING THAT THE CONSEQUENCES
OF YOUR OBEDIENCE ARE HIS
PROBLEM AND NOT YOURS.

My merciful Father, I claim and choose to believe Your Word that says that though You bring grief, You will show compassion, so great is Your unfailing love. You do not willingly bring affliction or grief to the children of men (Lam. 3:31–33).

Lord, according to Your Word, even when five sparrows were sold for two pennies, not one of them was forgotten by You. Indeed, the very hairs of my head are all numbered. Help me never to be afraid; I am worth far more to You than many sparrows (Luke 12:6–7).

Your anger lasts only a moment, Lord, but Your favor lasts a lifetime; weeping may remain for a night, but how I thank You that rejoicing comes in the morning (Ps. 30:5).

The ministry of the holy spirit is not just around, upon, and with believers but also inside believers.

Lord Jesus, You asked Your Father to give me a Counselor that would be with me forever—the Spirit of truth.

The world cannot accept the Holy Spirit, because it neither sees Him nor knows Him. But I know Him, for He lives with me and is in me.

You have not left me as an orphan. You came to me. Even though the world does not see You any more, I can see You through the work of Your Holy Spirit. Because You live, I also live.

Help me to realize that You, Jesus, are in Your Father, and I am in You, and You are in me (John 14:15–20).

GOD NEVER FORSAKES US. HE IS THE ONLY ONE WHO IS NOT REPELLED BY THE DEPTH AND LENGTH OF OUR NEEDS.

My Lord and Redeemer, when I did not know You, I was a slave to those who by nature are not gods. But now that I know You—or rather am known by You—I desperately do not want to turn back once again to those weak and miserable principles. Help me not to be enslaved by them all over again (Gal. 4:8–9).

Father, Your Word promises that the one who sows to please his sinful nature, from that nature will reap destruction, but the one who sows to please the Spirit, from the Spirit will reap eternal life (Gal. 6:8). Teach me and help me to sow to please the Spirit. By faith I eagerly await through the Spirit the righteousness for which I hope (Gal. 5:5).

GOD'S WORD DOES NOT SAY WE'LL
HAVE PEACE LIKE A POND BUT PEACE
LIKE A RIVER, RIGHTEOUSNESS LIKE
THE WAVES OF THE SEA.

Lord, I come to You in prayer, and I ask You now to let Your peace, God, which transcends all understanding, guard my heart and my mind in Christ Jesus (Phil. 4:7).

Help me not become weary in doing good, for at the proper time I will reap a harvest if I do not give up (Gal. 6:9).

Lord, when You bring this captive completely back to You, I will be like those who dream! My mouth will be filled with laughter and my tongue with songs of joy! The Lord has done great things for me, and I am filled with joy! (Ps. 126:1–3). You, O Lord, have filled my heart with greater joy than when my grain and new wine abound (Ps. 4:7).

THE RICHEST TESTIMONIES COME
FROM PEOPLE CHRIST HAS MADE
WHOLE AND WHO STILL REMEMBER
WHAT IT WAS LIKE TO BE BROKEN.

Lord, apart from You, there is no one righteous, not even one; there is no one who understands, no one who seeks You. All have turned away. We have together become worthless; there is no one who does good, not even one (Rom. 3:10–12).

The righteousness that comes from You comes through faith in Jesus Christ to all who believe. There is no difference, for all have sinned and fall short of Your glory, and are justified freely by Your grace through the redemption that came by Your Son, Christ Jesus (Rom. 3:22–23).

Help me to accept that Your gift of grace has never—and will never—be relegated by my ability to be good and righteous.

OUR BRIDEGROOM SOMETIMES LEADS
US TO DIFFICULT PLACES, BUT WE CAN
TRUST HIM TO HAVE PURPOSE IN OUR
STAY AND NEVER TO FORSAKE US.

I cry to You, Lord, in my trouble. Save
me from my distress (Ps. 107:13). I cry out
to You, God Most High, to You who fulfills
Your purpose for me. You send from heaven
and save me, rebuking those who hotly pursue
me. You send Your love and Your faithfulness
(Ps. 57:2–3).

You say to me, Lord, "My grace is sufficient for you, for my power is made perfect in
weakness." Therefore I will boast all the more
gladly about my weaknesses, so that Your power may rest on me (2 Cor. 12:9).

You will never leave me, Lord. Never will
You forsake me (Heb. 13:5). You are the only
absolute guarantee I have in all of life. Help me
cling to the one thing I can never lose.

WITH HANDS FRESHLY LOOSED, WE
FIND LIBERTY TO EMBRACE THE ONE
WHO NEVER CHANGES, AND COURAGE
TO RELEASE THOSE WHO WILL.

Lord God, forgive me my sins, for I also forgive everyone who sins against me. And lead me not into temptation (Luke 11:4). Lord, I confess to You that one of my greatest temptations is to refuse forgiveness to others. Please help me see the sober reality of Your will on this matter.

Help me to understand that the punishment and repercussions that come to people when they have done wrong is often sufficient for them. Instead of causing more grief, Your Word says I ought to forgive and comfort the person, so that he or she will not be overwhelmed by excessive sorrow (2 Cor. 2:7). Lord, help me to be the kind of person I'd want ministering to me after I had failed.

WE CAN EXPEND SO MUCH ENERGY
WHINING ABOUT OUR SITUATION
THAT WE HAVE NOTHING LEFT TO
INVEST IN THE REAL FIGHT.

O God, I will be glad and rejoice in Your love, for You saw my affliction and knew the anguish of my soul (Ps. 31:7).

Surely, Lord, You have granted me eternal blessings and made me glad with the joy of Your presence (Ps. 21:6). You turned my wailing into dancing; You removed my sackcloth and clothed me with joy that my heart may sing to You and not be silent. O Lord my God, I will give You thanks forever (Ps. 30:11–12).

Shout for joy, O heavens; rejoice, O earth; burst into song, O mountains! For the Lord comforts His people and will have compassion on His afflicted ones (Isa. 49:13).

BEFORE WE CAN GET CONTROLLING
THOUGHTS OUT OF OUR MINDS, THEY
MUST BECOME CHRIST-CONTROLLED
THOUGHTS WHILE THEY'RE INSIDE.

Lord God, one of the most important principles I will ever learn about life in the Spirit versus life in the flesh is found in Romans 8. Those who live according to the sinful nature have their minds set on what that nature desires; but those who live in accordance with the Spirit have their minds set on what the Spirit desires. The mind of sinful man is death, but the mind controlled by the Spirit is life and peace (Rom. 8:5–6).

Lord, the key to the Spirit-led life is my mind-set. Teach me to feed the Spirit and starve the flesh. Father God, through constant use of the solid food of Your Word, help me to train myself to distinguish good from evil (Heb. 5:14).

IF WE'RE GOING TO WIN OUR BATTLES, WE NEED TO WISE UP TO SOME OF SATAN'S SCHEMES AND PREPARE IN ADVANCE FOR VICTORY.

Though my enemy plots evil against me and devises wicked schemes, he will not succeed if I am walking with You, O God. You will make him turn his back when You aim at him with drawn bow. Be exalted, O Lord, in Your strength! I will sing and praise Your might! (Ps. 21:11–13).

Father, I joyfully celebrate the fact that one day, at the time of Your appearing, You will make my enemy like a fiery furnace. In Your wrath You will swallow him up, and Your fire will consume him (Ps. 21:9).

Lord God, I will shout for joy when You make me victorious, and I will lift up a banner in the name of my God! Please, Lord, grant these requests! (Ps. 20:5).

AUGUST

IF YOU DO YOUR PART FOR ONE
GENERATION, HE'LL DO HIS FOR
A THOUSAND. SOUNDS LIKE A
PRETTY GOOD DEAL TO ME.

Lord, I acknowledge that You are the "I AM." This is Your name forever, the name by which You are to be remembered from generation to generation (Exod. 3:14–15).

Father, help me to know that the Lord my God is God; You are the faithful God, keeping Your covenant of love to a thousand generations of those who love You and keep Your commands (Deut. 7:9).

The Lord my God is God of gods and Lord of lords, the great God, mighty and awesome. You show no partiality and accept no bribes (Deut. 10:17).

My Father, heaven is Your throne, and the earth is Your footstool (Isa. 66:1).

ASK GOD TO PERFORM WONDERS,
BUT ALWAYS KNOW THAT ULTIMATELY,
WE WILL BE MOST BLESSED WHEN
GOD IS MOST GLORIFIED.

Father, Your Word asks the question, "Does God give you His Spirit and work miracles among you because you observe the law, or because you believe what you heard?" (Gal. 3:5). The answer is because they believed what they heard. Help me to do likewise, Lord.

Christ Jesus, You spoke boldly to Your disciples with the promise, "If you have faith as small as a mustard seed, you can say to this mountain, 'Move from here to there' and it will move. Nothing will be impossible for you" (Matt. 17:20). Lord, develop in me the kind of faith that moves mountains in the power of Your Holy Spirit.

WE SIMPLY MUST FIND SATISFACTION IN GOD, BECAUSE DISSATISFACTION OR EMPTINESS WAVES A RED FLAG TO THE ENEMY.

Lord, Your Word is clear: wickedness suppresses truth. Your wrath will be revealed from heaven against all the godlessness and wickedness of men who suppress the truth by their wickedness (Rom. 1:18).

Father, Your Word also says that when people plant wickedness they will reap evil. You diagnose the root of the problem by saying that they have eaten the fruit of deception. These same people depend on their own strength and on many warriors (Hos. 10:13).

O God, please help me not to eat the fruit of deception. Cause me to recognize the rottenness of this "fruit," refusing to partake.

THE WORD OF GOD USES THE PHRASE "UNFAILING LOVE" THIRTY-TWO TIMES, AND NOT ONCE IS IT ATTRIBUTED TO HUMANS.

You, Lord, redeem Your servants; no one will be condemned who takes refuge in You (Ps. 34:22). When I said, "My foot is slipping," Your love supported me! When anxiety was great within me, Your consolation brought joy to my soul! (Ps. 94:18–19).

Your pleasure, O God, is not in the strength of the horse, nor Your delight in the legs of a man; You, O Lord, delight in those who fear You, who put their hope in Your unfailing love (Ps. 147:10–11). Help me to put my hope unreservedly in Your unfailing love!

I call to You and You save me. Even if I cry out in distress evening, morning, and noon, You never fail to hear my voice (Ps. 55:16–17).

THE PATH TO PEACE IS
PAVED WITH KNEEPRINTS.
BEND THE KNEE TO HIS
TRUSTWORTHY AUTHORITY.

Lord God, I desire to bow down to You in worship. I want to kneel before the Lord my Maker; for You are my God, and I am among the sheep of Your pasture, the flock under Your care (Ps. 95:6–7).

Though You, Lord, are on high, You look upon the lowly, but the proud You know from afar. Though I walk in the midst of trouble, You preserve my life; You stretch out Your hand against the anger of my foes, with Your right hand You save me.

You, Lord, will fulfill Your purpose for me; Your love endures forever—do not abandon the works of Your hands (Ps. 138:6–8).

I HAVE NOT ALWAYS FOUND MAN TRUSTWORTHY, BUT GOD HAS NEVER FAILED TO LIVE UP TO HIS WORD IN OUR RELATIONSHIP.

Jesus, teach me not to let my heart be troubled. Help me to trust in Your Father and also in You. In Your Father's house are many rooms; if it were not so, You would have told me. You have gone there to prepare a place for me. You will most assuredly come back and take me to be with You some day so that I may also be where You are (John 14:1–3).

For You are a merciful God; You will not abandon, destroy me, or forget the covenant with my spiritual forefathers, which You confirmed to them by oath (Deut. 4:31). I belong to Jesus Christ; therefore I, too, am Abraham's seed and an heir according to Your promise (Gal. 3:29). Like Isaac was, I am a child of promise (Gal. 4:28).

TO REMOVE THE OBSTACLE OF PRIDE, WE MUST VIEW IT AS A BITTER ENEMY AND VIEW HUMILITY AS A DEAR FRIEND.

God, according to Your steadfast Word, pride only breeds quarrels, but wisdom is found in those who take advice (Prov. 13:10). My pride has caused such conflict, Lord! Please help me to humble myself and receive Your wisdom!

I desire to humble myself before You and trust that You will lift me up (James 4:10), for You have promised to sustain the humble but cast the wicked to the ground (Ps. 147:6).

Lord God, Your might brings down rulers from their thrones but lifts up the humble (Luke 1:52). Please help me to listen to advice and accept instruction so that in the end I will be wise (Prov. 19:20).

SLAVERY IS ANYTHING THAT KEEPS YOU FROM YOUR GOD-ORDAINED DESTINY AND THE FULFILLMENT OF HIS PROMISES TO YOU.

Lord, Your Word says that when I offer myself to someone or something to obey as a slave, I am a slave to the one whom I obey, whether I am a slave to sin, which leads to death, or to obedience, which leads to righteousness (Rom. 6:16). O Father, I deeply desire to be a slave to righteousness!

God, I have died to the law through the body of Christ so that I might belong to another, to Him who was raised from the dead. You saved me in order that I might bear fruit to You (Rom. 7:4).

Thank You in advance, my Father, that You are going to use my life and cause it to bear fruit!

ORDINARILY, THE PRIMARY HINDRANCE TO SATISFACTION IN OUR LIVES IS REFUSING HIM ACCESS TO OUR EMPTY PLACES.

Lord, please help me not to miss the grace of God. Help me to see to it that no bitter root grows up in me to cause trouble and defile many (Heb. 12:15).

Search me, O God, and know my heart; test me and know my anxious thoughts. See if there is any offensive way in me, and lead me in the way everlasting (Ps. 139:23–24).

Lord God, help me to guard the good deposit that was entrusted to me. I must guard it with the help of the Holy Spirit who lives in me (2 Tim. 1:14). Help me to put on Your full armor so that I can take my stand against the devil's schemes (Eph. 6:11).

Just as memory is a vital part of the learning process, it is also a vital part of the faith-building process.

Lord, according to Your Word, he who conceals his sins does not prosper, but whoever confesses and renounces them finds mercy (Prov. 28:13). Lord, I remember the height from which I have fallen. I repent and deeply desire to do the things I did at first. I know that if I do not repent, You will come to me and remove any light my life has in this dark world (Rev. 2:5).

So, thank You, God, for disciplining me for my good, that I may share in Your holiness (Heb. 12:10). Thank You for assuring me in Your Word that the ones You rebuke and discipline are the ones You love. To the best of my knowledge, I have been earnest and repentant (Rev. 3:19).

WE DON'T HAVE TO HANG OUR
HEADS TO BE HUMBLE. WE HUMBLE
OURSELVES SIMPLY BY SUBMITTING
TO HIS GREATNESS EVERY DAY.

Lord, I pray that one day I will begin to consider my precious losses gains for the sake of Christ as You use my suffering, my life, and my testimony. Whatever was to my profit I now consider loss for the sake of Christ.

What is more, I consider everything a loss compared to the surpassing greatness of knowing Christ Jesus my Lord, for whose sake I have lost all things.

I want to gain You, Christ, and be found in You, not having a righteousness of my own that comes from the law, but that which is through faith in You—the righteousness that comes from God and is by faith (Phil. 3:7–9).

THE ENEMY SPECIALIZES IN TAKING
ADVANTAGE OF ANY REFUSAL TO
FORGIVE. ASK GOD IF YOU ARE IN
ANY WAY PERPETUATING DIVISION.

Lord, You tell me to forgive others in the sight of Christ in order that Satan might not outwit me. Help me never to be unaware of his schemes (2 Cor. 2:11). Please help me to see how much the enemy takes advantage of unforgiveness. I offer him a foothold any time I refuse to forgive.

Lord, my conscience is clear, but that does not make me innocent. It is You who judges me. Therefore I am to judge nothing before the appointed time; Your Word tells me to wait until You come. You will bring to light what is hidden in darkness and will expose the motives of men's hearts. At that time each will receive his praise from God (1 Cor. 4:4–5).

No matter what our strongholds have been, God can plant us deeply in His love and grow us by the water of His word.

Your Word declares that we will be called oaks of righteousness, a planting of the Lord for the display of His splendor. We will rebuild the ancient ruins and restore the places long devastated; we will renew the ruined cities that have been devastated for generations (Isa. 61:3b–4).

I will find joy in You, my Lord. You will cause me to ride on the heights of the land and to feast on the inheritance You have given my spiritual forefathers (Isa. 58:14).

Now is my time of grief, but I will see You again and I will rejoice, and no one will take away my joy. In that day I will no longer ask You anything. I can ask and I will receive, and my joy will be complete (John 16:22–24).

AS A CHILD AND A JOINT HEIR WITH CHRIST, REFUSE THE ENEMY A SINGLE INCH OF THE GROUND YOU ARE TAKING BACK.

Father, help me, enable me, strengthen me to put to death whatever belongs to my earthly nature: sexual immorality, impurity, lust, evil desires and greed, which is idolatry. Because of these, Your wrath is coming. I used to walk in these ways, in the life I once lived (Col. 3:5). Lord, help me to understand that "putting to death" means to cease empowering it or fueling it or doing things that arouse it to unholy life.

Thank You for promising that no temptation has seized me except what is common to man. You are faithful; You will not let me be tempted beyond what I can bear. But when I am tempted You will also provide a way out so that I can stand up under it (I Cor. 10:13).

WE DON'T BECOME VICTORS BY CONQUERING THE ENEMY BUT THROUGH SURRENDER TO CHRIST, THROUGH DEPENDENCE ON GOD.

I love You, O Lord, my strength! You are my Rock, my Fortress, and my Deliverer; You, my God, are my Rock, in whom I take refuge. You are my Shield and the horn of my salvation, my Stronghold! I call to You, O Lord, who is worthy of praise, and I am saved from my enemies! (Ps. 18:1–3).

You, O Lord, keep my lamp burning; You turn my darkness into light. With Your help I can advance against a troop; with You, my God, I can scale a wall!

As for You, my God, Your way is perfect; Your Word is flawless. You are a shield for all who take refuge in You (Ps. 18:28–30).

ALLOW YOUR CIRCUMSTANCES AND WEAKNESSES TO DO THE JOB GOD HAS SENT THEM TO DO— PROVOKE HUMILITY.

Do not be far from me, Lord, for trouble is near and there is no one to help. . . . They feel like roaring lions tearing their prey open, their mouths wide against me (Ps. 22:11, 13).

But to You, O Lord, I lift up my soul; in You I trust, O my God. Do not let me be put to shame, nor let my enemies triumph over me (Ps. 25:1–2).

Guard my life and rescue me, O Lord. Let me not be put to shame, for I take refuge in You. May integrity and uprightness protect me, because my hope is in You (Ps. 25:20–21).

THE HEALTHIEST CHRISTIANS YOU
WILL EVER MEET ARE THOSE WHO
TAKE A DAILY DOSE OF GOD'S WORD
AND CHOOSE TO BELIEVE IT WORKS.

You, my God, have put Your words in my mouth and covered me with the shadow of Your hand—You who set the heavens in place, who laid the foundations of the earth, and who say to Zion, "You are my people" (Isa. 51:16).

Lord, You rule forever by Your power, Your eyes watch the nations—let not the rebellious rise up against You (Ps. 66:7). The fool says in his heart, "There is no God" (Ps. 14:1).

Lord, please help me to revere Your name. You have promised that, if I do, the sun of righteousness will rise with healing in its wings and that I will go out and leap like a calf released from the stall (Mal. 4:2).

OUR PURPOSE FOR EXISTENCE IS
TO PLEASE GOD. SO IF WE DON'T
EXERCISE FAITH, WE WILL NEVER
FULFILL OUR REASON FOR BEING.

Lord, You have told us in Your Word that in the last days many will turn away from the faith and will betray and hate one another (Matt. 24:10). O Father, please help me never turn away and turn cold.

Lord, You asked in Your Word, "When the Son of Man comes, will He find faith on the earth?" (Luke 18:8). You search the world over for people with faith. Make me one of them, Lord. Find faith in me.

Merciful God, thank You for opening my eyes and turning them from darkness to light, and from the power of Satan to God, so that I may receive forgiveness of sins and a place among those who are sanctified by faith in You (Acts 26:18).

BELIEVING GOD CLOSES THE GAP
BETWEEN OUR THEOLOGY AND OUR
REALITY. IT DOESN'T SO MUCH MAKE
US WHAT WE ARE BUT HOW WE ARE.

Father, Your Word asks, "How can you believe if you accept praise from one another, yet make no effort to obtain the praise that comes from the only God?" (John 5:44). Please help me to make every effort to obtain the praise that comes from You, Lord. I cannot obtain this praise from You without belief.

Father, how I thank You for the faith You have given me. Before this faith came, I was held prisoner by the law, locked up until faith was revealed (Gal. 3:23).

Mighty God, help me to understand that I've been called by You to walk by faith and not by sight (2 Cor. 5:7). Strengthen my spiritual vision, Lord!

MAKING A REASONABLE AND LIVABLE LIFESTYLE OF BELIEVING AND SPEAKING GOD'S WORD IS LIKE LIVING ON THE CPR OF THE HOLY SPIRIT.

Christ Jesus, You said emphatically, "I tell you the truth, anyone who has faith in me will do what I have been doing." In fact, You said, "He will do even greater things than these, because I am going to the Father" (John 14:12).

Father, Your Word asks the question, "Does God give you His Spirit and work miracles among you because you observe the law, or because you believe what you heard?" (Gal. 3:5). The answer is because they believed what they heard. Help me to do likewise, Lord.

Father, I have been called for Your name's sake to the obedience that comes from faith (Rom. 1:5). Please help me to understand that obedience demands faith.

We accomplish little good when we tell of the praiseworthy deeds of the Lord but live lives inconsistent with his truth.

Lord God, according to Your Word, we purify ourselves by obeying the truth. This purification frees us to have sincere love for our brothers, loving one another deeply, from the heart (1 Pet. 1:22).

This love, You tell us, does not delight in evil but rejoices with the truth (1 Cor. 13:6). Help me, Lord, to possess a genuine and godly love for others and to rejoice with the truth.

Your Word also exhorts us that if one of us should wander from the truth, someone should bring him back (James 5:19). Please bring strong believers into my life so that we may be mutually encouraged by one another's faith (Rom. 1:12).

SURROUNDED BY A SOCIETY THAT SPOUTS MANY GODS BUT, AT BEST, NOBLY AGREES TO EQUATE THEM, YOU AND I CAN KNOW THE LORD IS GOD.

Father God, like the children of Israel in the prophet Jeremiah's day, I live in the midst of deception; in their deceit many people refuse to acknowledge You (Jer. 9:6). Please help me not to be taken captive by the deception that surrounds me in this society.

You have warned me in Your Word not to believe every spirit but to test the spirits to see whether they are from God, because many false prophets have gone out into the world (1 John 4:1). Help me to be discerning of messengers with false visions and deceptive divinations: the ones who say, "The Lord declares," though You, the Lord, have not sent them (Ezek. 13:6). O God, as You increase my belief, teach me also what not to believe.

PRAYING THE SCRIPTURE FUELS OUR FAITH IN THE ONE WHO IS FAITHFUL. IT FUELS OUR BELIEF IN THE ONE WHO IS BELIEVABLE.

Father God, how great is the love You have lavished on me, that I should be called a child of God! And that is what I am! (I John 3:1).

As I walk with You, Lord, You will not let my foot slip—You who watch over me will not slumber; indeed, You who watch over Your children will neither slumber nor sleep.

You, the Lord, watch over me—You are my shade at my right hand; the sun will not harm me by day nor the moon by night. You, Lord God, will keep me from all harm—You will watch over my life; You will watch over my coming and going both now and forevermore (Ps. 121:3–8).

What a comfort to know that the places God chooses to lead us always flow out of his unfailing love.

You, my faithful Lord, are gracious and compassionate, slow to anger and rich in love. You, my Lord, are good to all; You have compassion on all You have made. All You have made will praise You, O Lord; Your saints will extol You (Ps. 145:8–10).

Lord, how I thank You for showing Your love to me by sending Your one and only Son into the world that I might live through Him. This is love: not that I loved You, but that You loved me and sent Your Son as an atoning sacrifice for my sins (1 John 4:9–10).

Lord, my God, may Your unfailing love be my comfort, according to Your promise to Your servant (Ps. 119:76).

BOTH BLESSING AND JOY COME TO US THROUGH OBEDIENCE, OFTEN IN TIMES OF PERSECUTION AND PAIN.

Merciful Savior, according to Your Word, I am blessed when men hate me, when they exclude me and insult me and reject me as evil, because of You, the Son of Man. Your Word says I have cause to rejoice in that day and leap for joy, because great is my reward in heaven. For that is how their fathers treated the prophets (Luke 6:22–23).

Therefore help me set my face like flint, and I know I will not be put to shame. He who vindicates me is near. Who then will bring charges against me? Let us face each other! Who is my accuser? Let him confront me! It is the Sovereign Lord who helps me. Who is he that will condemn me? (Isa. 50:7b–9a).

GOD WILL SOMETIMES ALLOW THINGS TO GET BAD ENOUGH THAT WE WILL BE FORCED TO LOOK UP.

My Lord and my Creator, I confess to you that I, like everyone else in the human condition, am weak in my natural self. I used to offer the parts of my body in slavery to impurities. I have also personally experienced the ever-increasing nature of wickedness (Rom. 6:19).

But no matter what I've tried to tell myself, my addictions will only grow worse without Your absolute intervention. Thank You, Father, that no matter how I've been enslaved, You can set me free!

Father, I thank You in advance that I am going to be set free from this sin and I can become a slave to You, reaping glorious benefits that lead to holiness! (Rom. 6:22).

GOD DOES NOT ALLOW HIS PEOPLE TO BE OPPRESSED SO THAT THEY WILL BE DEFEATED BUT SO THAT THEY WILL ULTIMATELY BE VICTORIOUS.

Lord, no matter what kind of suffering my sins have caused me, I thank You that my present sufferings are not worth comparing with the glory that will be revealed in me (Rom. 8:18).

Father, what glorious news that You foreknew me and all my struggles, and yet You also predestined me to be conformed to the likeness of Your Son, that He might be the firstborn among many brothers! (Rom. 8:29).

God, how I thank You that I can confidently claim that if You are for me, who can be against me? (Rom. 8:31). As Your child, help me to realize every day of my life that You are for me and never against me.

We have little defense against the destructive nature of the enemy without the power of God working in our favor.

Lord God, according to Your Word, where there is no revelation, the people cast off restraint (Prov. 29:18). O Father, help me to understand that I have no power of restraint or self-control without Your Word made alive in me by Your Holy Spirit!

How long will I turn Your glory into shame, O Lord? How long will I love delusions and seek false gods? (Ps. 4:2). Expose the delusions and false gods in my life, O Lord, and set me free!

Lord God, I pray You will give me the desire of my heart, which at this moment is to be free. Make all my plans succeed (Ps. 20:4).

When you're feeling unlovely, soak yourself in the proclamations of God's unfailing love for you.

Father, in many ways I have been like the prodigal son, squandering my inheritance on worthless living.

Yet while I was still a long way off, You saw me and were filled with compassion for me. You ran to receive me back into Your arms. I have come to You to confess my sin against heaven and against You.

I have felt unworthy to be called Your son. But You celebrated my return to You and desired to put Your best robe around me and Your ring on my finger. Because of Your great mercy, You've received me back as a child, not a servant. I felt dead, but now I feel alive again! (Luke 15:13, 20–23, 32).

CAN YOU THINK OF ANY NEED YOU HAVE THAT WOULD REQUIRE MORE STRENGTH THAN GOD EXERCISED TO RAISE THE DEAD?

Father God, I commit myself and my suffering to You, my faithful Creator, and I will continue to do good (1 Pet. 4:19). For I know whom I have believed, and am convinced that You are able to guard what I have entrusted to You for that day (2 Tim. 1:12).

Oh, that my words were recorded, that they were written on a scroll, that they were inscribed with an iron tool on lead, or engraved in rock forever!

I know that You, my Redeemer, live, and that in the end You will stand upon the earth. And after my skin has been destroyed, yet in my flesh I will see You, God. I myself will see You with my own eyes. . . . How my heart yearns within me! (Job 19:23–27).

WE CAN LIVE OUR ENTIRE LIVES AS CHRISTIANS AND NEVER FULFILL THE GLORIOUS PLAN GOD TAILORED FOR US IN ADVANCE.

Lord, I do not want to be like those who refuse to pay attention to You. Please help me not to turn my back in stubbornness and stop up my ears just because Your will is hard at times. Help me not to make my heart as hard as flint and refuse to listen to the words that You, Lord Almighty, have sent by Your Spirit (Zech. 7:11–12).

Lord God, empower me to make every effort to live in peace with all men and to be holy; without holiness no one will see the Lord. Help me to see to it that I don't miss the grace of God and that no bitter root grows up to cause trouble and defile many (Heb. 12:14–15).

SEPTEMBER

NO MATTER WHAT TIME OF NIGHT YOU ROLL OVER IN BED, YOU WILL CATCH GOD IN THE MIDDLE OF A THOUGHT ABOUT YOU.

Do not gloat over me, my enemy! Though I have fallen, I will rise. Though I sit in darkness, the Lord will be my light (Mic. 7:8).

Lord, according to Your Word, the light shines in the darkness, but the darkness has not understood it (John 1:5). Because I'm Yours, help me to see that Your light is shining in my darkness whether or not I can behold it or understand it.

Lord, You have come into the world as a light, so that no one who believes in You should stay in darkness (John 12:46). You are like the light of morning at sunrise on a cloudless morning, like the brightness after rain that brings the grass from the earth (2 Sam. 23:4).

GOD'S WORD IS FULL OF HIS
PROCLAMATIONS OF LOVE FOR YOU.
YOU CAN HEAR HIM TELL YOU HE
LOVES YOU EVERY TIME YOU OPEN IT.

Lord Jesus, You Yourself bore my sins in Your body on the tree, so that I might die to sins and live for righteousness; by Your wounds I have been healed. For I was like a sheep going astray, but now I have returned to the Shepherd and Overseer of my soul (I Pet. 2:24–25).

Lord God, cause my heart, soul, and mind to be so overtaken by Your grace that I share the testimony of the sinful woman who anointed Your feet. You said of her, "I tell you, her many sins have been forgiven—for she loved much. But he who has been forgiven little loves little" (Luke 7:47).

Lord Jesus, make our story a love story.

THE MORE WE KNOW THE WORD,
THE QUICKER WE RECOGNIZE WHAT
IS SETTING ITSELF UP AGAINST
THE KNOWLEDGE OF GOD.

Turn Your ear to me, O Lord. Come quickly to my rescue; be my rock of refuge, a strong fortress to save me. Since You are my Rock and my Fortress, for the sake of Your name lead and guide me (Ps. 31:2–3).

I trust in You, O Lord; I say, "You are my God." My times are in Your hands; deliver me from my enemies and those who pursue me. Let Your face shine on Your servant; save me in Your unfailing love. Let me not be put to shame, O Lord, for I have cried out to you (Ps. 31:14–17).

I celebrate the fact that You, the God of peace, will soon crush Satan under Your feet, and until then the grace of our Lord Jesus Christ is with us (Rom. 16:20).

EVEN IF WE'VE DRAINED ALL
THE HUMAN RESOURCES AROUND
US DRY, HE IS OUR INEXHAUSTIBLE
WELL OF LIVING WATER.

Lord, Your Word is right and true; You are faithful in all You do. You love righteousness and justice. I thank You that the earth is full of Your unfailing love! (Ps. 33:4–5).

You are not a man, that You should lie, not a son of man, that You should change Your mind. I thank You that when You speak, You act. And what You promise, You fulfill (Num. 23:19). I will exalt You and praise Your name, for in perfect faithfulness You have done marvelous things planned long ago (Isa. 25:1).

Now to the King eternal, immortal, invisible, the only God, be honor and glory for ever and ever. Amen (1 Tim. 1:17).

WE MAY WANT A DAILY DOSE OF DRAMATICS, BUT GOD ENJOYS SEEING THE PROVEN FAITHFULNESS OF SIMPLE DAILY DEVOTION.

Father, according to Your Word, a man can't accurately claim to have faith if he has no deeds. Faith by itself, if it is not accompanied by action, is dead. Faith and actions work together (James 2:14, 17, 22).

Cause my faith to be evidenced by my deeds, Lord God. I acknowledge that my faith is made complete by what I do (James 2:22). Faith works!

O Lord, I want You to be able to say of me, "I know your deeds, your love and faith, your service and perseverance, and that you are now doing more than you did at first" (Rev. 2:19). Cause these words to be true of my life, dear Father.

IN THE SAME WAY THAT SIN QUENCHES THE HOLY SPIRIT WITHIN US, SCRIPTURE QUICKENS THE HOLY SPIRIT WITHIN US.

Father, I acknowledge that at times in my life I've fed on ashes instead of Your Word and let my deluded heart mislead me. Help me recognize when the thing I'm holding onto for security is a lie (Isa. 44:20).

Your Word says, "Woe to those who draw sin along with cords of deceit, and wickedness as with cart ropes" (Isa. 5:18). Please make me instantly aware the moment I am tempted to pick up a cord of deceit.

My faithful God, help me to see to it that no one takes me captive through hollow and deceptive philosophy, which depends on human tradition and the basic principles of this world rather than on Christ (Col. 2:8).

GOD NEVER FORGETS HIS PROMISES.
IN TURN, HE INTENDS FOR HIS
CHILDREN NEVER TO FORGET HIS
FAITHFULNESS TO FULFILL THEM.

Lord God, it is because You love me and keep Your Word that You brought me out with a mighty hand and redeemed me from the land of slavery, from the power of the pharaoh of this world. Help me to absolutely know therefore that You, the Lord my God, are God; You are the faithful God, keeping Your covenant of love to a thousand generations of those who love You and keep Your commands (Deut. 7:8–9).

Lord, I have the assurance of Your Word that after I have suffered a little while, You, the God of all grace who called me to Your eternal glory in Christ, will restore me and make me strong, firm, and steadfast (1 Pet. 5:10).

FREEDOM BECOMES REALITY WHEN
WE YIELD TO THE AUTHORITY OF
GOD. WE ARE FILLED WITH THE SPIRIT
AS WE YIELD TO HIS LORDSHIP.

Lord Jesus, You have promised that the Holy Spirit, whom the Father sent in Your name, will teach Your disciples all things and will remind those who follow You of everything You have said in Your Word.

Peace You leave with me; Your peace You give me. You do not give to me as the world gives. My heart need not be troubled or afraid (John 14:26–27).

Since ancient times no one has heard, no ear has perceived, no eye has seen any God besides You, who acts on behalf of those who wait for Him. You come to the aid of those who gladly do right, who remember Your ways (Isa. 64:4–5). Empower me to live obediently through Your Holy Spirit!

OUR LIBERATION IS A REALITY ONLY
IN THE PLACES OF OUR LIVES WHERE
THE FREE SPIRIT OF GOD IS RELEASED,
WHERE HE IS IN CONTROL.

Father, according to Your Word, it is better not to eat meat or drink wine or to do anything else that will cause a brother or sister to fall (Rom. 14:21). I pray that not only will I be mindful of this exhortation with others but that You will cause those around me not to do things that will cause me to fall!

Father, Your Word says that it is for freedom that Christ has set us free. With all my heart I desire to stand firm, then, and not let myself be burdened again by a yoke of slavery (Gal. 5:1).

Lord, I am helpless on my own. Empower me with the strength of Your Holy Spirit. Please help me, Lord!

HUMILITY IS NOT SOMETHING WE HAVE UNTIL HUMBLING OURSELVES IS SOMETHING WE DO.

Thank You, God, for choosing me in Christ before the creation of the world to be holy and blameless in Your sight (Eph. 1:4).

By Your grace, Lord, I have been saved, through faith—and this is not from myself, it is the gift of God—not by works, so that I cannot boast (Eph. 2:8–9). Therefore, as it is written: "Let him who boasts boast in the Lord" (1 Cor. 1:31).

I am one of Your chosen people, O God. I acknowledge and accept as fact that I am holy and dearly loved. In response, help me to clothe myself with compassion, kindness, humility, gentleness, and patience (Col. 3:12).

In between dramatic revelations, what's a believer to do? The day-in, day-out fundamentals, that's what.

Although my sins testify against me, O Lord, do something for the sake of Your name. For my backsliding is great; I have sinned against You (Jer. 14:7). O Lord, I acknowledge my wickedness and guilt. I have indeed sinned against You (Jer. 14:20).

If You, O Lord, kept a record of sins, O Lord, who could stand? But with You there is forgiveness; therefore You are feared. I wait for You, Lord. My soul waits, and in Your Word I put my hope. My soul waits for You, Lord, more than watchmen wait for the morning. With You, Lord, is unfailing love and with You is full redemption. You Yourself will redeem me from all my sins (Ps. 130:3–8).

GOD DELIGHTS TO HEAR THE
PETITIONS OF THOSE WHO WANT
HIM MORE THAN THEY WANT
ANYTHING ELSE HE COULD GIVE.

O Lord, how priceless is Your unfailing love! Both high and low among men find refuge in the shadow of Your wings. They feast on the abundance of Your house; You give them drink from Your river of delights. For with You is the fountain of life; in Your light we see light (Ps. 36:7–9).

One thing I ask of You, Lord, this is what I seek: that I may dwell in the house of the Lord all the days of my life, to gaze upon Your beauty and to seek You in Your temple. For in the day of trouble You will keep me safe in Your dwelling; You will hide me in the shelter of Your tabernacle and set me high upon a rock (Ps. 27:4–5).

THANK GOD THAT, ALTHOUGH YOU
CANNOT CHANGE THE PAST, HE CAN
HELP YOU CHANGE WHAT YOU'RE
DOING WITH IT.

I want to know You, Jesus, and the power
of Your resurrection and fellowship of sharing
in Your sufferings, becoming like You in Your
death. Not that I have already obtained all this,
or have already been made perfect, but I press
on to take hold of that for which You, Christ
Jesus, took hold of me.

I do not consider myself yet to have taken
hold of it. But one thing I do: forgetting what
is behind and straining toward what is ahead,
I press on toward the goal to win the prize for
which God has called me heavenward in You,
Christ Jesus (Phil. 3:7–14).

Your Word is simply telling me not to live
in the past and fail to embrace the future You
have for me.

OUR WORDS ARE POTENT NO
MATTER HOW WE USE THEM, BUT
WHAT WOULD HAPPEN IF WE LET
GOD TAKE HOLD OF THEM?

If I speak in the tongues of men and of angels but have not love, I am only a resounding gong or a clanging cymbal.

If I have the gift of prophecy and can fathom all mysteries and all knowledge, and if I have a faith that can move mountains, but have not love, I am nothing.

If I give all I possess to the poor and surrender my body to the flames, but have not love, I gain nothing (1 Cor. 13:1–3).

God, through the power of Your Holy Spirit, help me to live in harmony with others, be sympathetic, love as a brother or sister, be compassionate and humble (1 Pet. 3:8). For You oppose the proud but give grace to the humble (James 4:6).

VICTORY ALWAYS BEGINS WITH A CRY
FOR HELP. WHEN WE COME TO THE
END OF OURSELVES AND CRY OUT
FOR HELP, AMAZING THINGS HAPPEN.

Victorious Lord, I am not silenced by the darkness, by the thick darkness that covers my face (Job 23:17). I will cry out to You, Lord God, and I will rebuke the enemy that seeks to devour me.

Lord, when I hoped for good, evil came; when I looked for light, then came darkness (Job 30:26). Help me, Lord, for hope deferred has made my heart sick (Prov. 13:12). Help me to put my hope in You.

Lord God, say to this captive, "Come out," and to this child in darkness, "Be free!" Good Shepherd, cause me to find pasture even on every barren hill (Isa. 49:9).

BELIEVE HIM. BELIEVE HE CAN
DO WHAT HE SAYS HE CAN DO.
AND BELIEVE ALSO THAT YOU CAN
DO WHAT HE SAYS YOU CAN DO.

Lord God, when I was dead in my sins and in the uncircumcision of my sinful nature, You made me alive with Christ. You forgave me all my sins, having canceled the written code, with its regulations, that was against me and that stood opposed to me; You took it away, nailing it to Christ's cross.

And having disarmed the powers and authorities, You made a public spectacle of them, triumphing over them by the cross (Col. 2:13–15).

You, my God, made Your Son, Jesus Christ, who had no sin, to be sin for me, so that in Him I might become the righteousness of God (2 Cor. 5:21).

THE REASON MOST OF OUR
BELIEF SYSTEMS AREN'T WORKING
IS BECAUSE THEY ARE BIG ON
SYSTEMS AND SMALL ON BELIEF.

O God, Your chariots are tens of thousands and thousands of thousands! The Lord has come into His sanctuary.

Praise be to the Lord, to God my Savior, who daily bears my burdens. My God is a God who saves; from the Sovereign Lord comes escape from death (Ps. 68:17, 19–20).

Father, allow my eyes to see the defeat of my adversary. Let my ears hear the rout of my wicked foe (Ps. 92:11). Cause me to still bear fruit in old age . . . proclaiming, "The Lord is upright; he is my rock, and there is no wickedness in him" (Ps. 92:14–15).

Lord, I have heard of Your fame; I stand in awe of Your deeds. Renew them in our day, in our time make them known (Hab. 3:2).

I HAVE PUT THE DEVIL ON ALERT. HE
MAY MAKE MY LIFE VERY DIFFICULT
BUT HE CANNOT MAKE ME QUIT, FOR I
AM ONE OF GOD'S DEAR CHILDREN.

You, Father, are my loving God and my
fortress, my stronghold and my deliverer, my
shield, in whom I take refuge, who subdues
people under me (Ps. 144:2). Help me never
to worship any other god, for You, my Lord,
are a jealous God (Exod. 20:4–5).

You placed all things under the feet of my
Savior, Jesus Christ, and appointed Him to be
head over everything for the church, which is
His body, the fullness of Him who fills everything in every way! (Eph. 1:22–23).

You alone are my rock and my salvation;
You are my fortress, I will not be shaken. My
salvation and my honor depend on You; You
are my mighty rock, my refuge (Ps. 62:6–7).

GOD IS NOT A MAN. HE DOES NOT
SIMPLY RESIST IGNOBLE TENDENCIES.
HE LACKS THEM ALTOGETHER. YOU
CAN TAKE HIM AT HIS WORD.

O, Lord, You have made everything beautiful in Your time. You have also set eternity in the hearts of men; yet we cannot fathom what You have done from beginning to end (Eccles. 3:11).

You are slow to anger and great in power; You will not leave the guilty unpunished. Your way is in the whirlwind and the storm, my Lord, and clouds are the dust of Your feet (Nah. 1:3).

Father, I acknowledge that Your thoughts are not my thoughts, neither are Your ways my ways. As the heavens are higher than the earth, so are Your ways higher than my ways and Your thoughts than my thoughts (Isa. 55:8–9).

We don't achieve victory once, then never have to bother with it again. Desiring to be godly is the work of a lifetime.

Father, Your Word says that the love of money is a root of all kinds of evil. Please help me not be eager for money and take the chance of wandering from the faith and piercing myself with many griefs (1 Tim. 6:10).

Help me to flee the evil desires of youth, and pursue righteousness, faith, love, and peace, along with those who call on the Lord out of a pure heart (2 Tim. 2:22). You want me to pursue faith, not just sit back and wait until it develops.

O Father, help me to fight the good fight, holding on to faith and a good conscience. Please don't let me be like some who have rejected these and so have shipwrecked their faith (1 Tim. 1:18–19).

WE CAN'T BELIEVE GOD IN
OUR DAY-TO-DAY CHALLENGES IF
WE ARE NOT PRESENTLY AND
ACTIVELY IN HIS WORD.

Father, Your Word says that faith comes from hearing the message, and the message is heard through the Word of Christ (Rom. 10:17). Cause me to continue to listen to Your Word! Without Your Word, my faith will never grow.

Lord, according to Scripture, the Word is near me; it is in my mouth and in my heart, and it is the word of faith I am proclaiming (Rom. 10:8).

You don't want me to be persuaded just by the wise and persuasive words of men but by the demonstration of the Spirit's power, so that my faith will not rest on men's wisdom, but on God's power (1 Cor. 2:4–5).

IF IN OUR PURSUIT OF KNOWLEDGE GOD HAS GOTTEN SMALLER, WE HAVE BEEN DECEIVED, NO MATTER HOW INTELLIGENT THE DECEIVER.

Father God, I acknowledge that the Spirit clearly says that in later times some will abandon the faith and follow deceiving spirits and things taught by demons (I Tim. 4:1).

As the time of Your return approaches, there will be increasing deception and literally twisted doctrines that are being taught by angels of darkness.

Please develop a higher level of discernment in me, Jesus. Help me to know truth so well that I will quickly recognize the most finely crafted lie.

Lord God, help me to keep up my courage and have faith in You that things will happen just as You said (Acts 27:25).

WHAT HEARTBREAK WE MUST BRING
TO GOD WHEN WE CONTINUE TO
DISBELIEVE HIS LOVE? WHAT MORE
COULD HE HAVE SAID OR DONE?

Long before You became flesh, Lord, and dwelled among us (John 1:14), the Word of God prophesied that You would take up our infirmities and carry our sorrows. Yet the people You came to save considered You stricken by God, smitten by God, and afflicted.

But You were pierced for our transgressions, You were crushed for our iniquities; the punishment that brought us peace was upon You, and by Your wounds we are healed (Isa. 53:4–5).

Savior Jesus, I do not have the proper words of gratitude for all You were willing to do for me to be saved. How can I doubt Your love for me after all that You so willingly did?

WE HAVE NO HOPE WHATSOEVER OF GOD'S BEING RECOGNIZABLE IN US IF THE SPIRIT OF CHRIST DOES NOT DWELL IN US.

Lord God, I have heard the slander of many; at times there is terror on every side; I sometimes feel that others conspire against me and the enemy plots to take my life.

But I trust in You, O Lord; I say, "You are my God." My times are in Your hands; deliver me from my enemies and from those who pursue me. Let Your face shine on Your servant; save me in Your unfailing love (Ps. 31:13–16).

How I thank You, Lord, for having the power to turn any curse into a blessing for me, because You, the Lord my God, love me (Deut. 23:5).

GOD'S UNFAILING LOVE ALSO APPEARS IN HIS UNWILLINGNESS TO ALLOW REBELLION TO GO UNNOTICED AND UNDISCIPLINED.

Father, according to Your Word, if any person is caught in a sin, someone who is spiritual should restore him gently. Your Word also says that even the spiritual believer must be very alert because he or she may also be tempted (Gal. 6:1).

Father, I pray for those You are putting in my path to help me. I pray for their protection as well as my own. I also pray that I will know when I am strong enough to help others. When that time comes, I pray that You will cause me to be absolutely alert so that I do not fall to temptation.

Lord, since I live by the Spirit, help me to keep in step with the Spirit (Gal. 5:25).

Trying to ignore satan doesn't work for very long, especially if you're beginning to be a threat to his dark kingdom.

Father God, please help me to keep in mind that my struggle is not against flesh and blood, but against the rulers, against the authorities, against the powers of this dark world and against the spiritual forces of evil in the heavenly realms (Eph. 6:12).

Help me to be self-controlled and alert, for I know my enemy the devil prowls around like a roaring lion looking for someone to devour (1 Pet. 5:8).

My faithful Father, whether I turn to the right or to the left, cause my ears to hear a voice behind me saying, "This is the way; walk in it" (Isa. 30:21).

THE JOY THAT RESULTS FROM
WALKING IN TRUTH IS NOT JUST
GOD'S BUT OURS. THOSE WHO WALK
IN TRUTH WALK IN LIBERTY.

Lord God, one reason You inspired Your Word to be written was so that I, Your dear child, could know that my sins are forgiven on account of Your good name (1 John 2:12). I can be strong because the Word of God lives in me, and in You I have overcome the evil one (1 John 2:14).

Lord Jesus, I acknowledge that You, the Son of Man, have authority on earth to forgive sins! (Luke 5:24). Please help me to understand that when I doubt Your forgiveness after my own repentance, in effect, I'm saying I can do my part but You cannot do Yours. Forgive me, Jesus, and help me not to minimize Your sovereign authority to complete this awesome, redemptive work.

FAITH IS NOT BELIEVING IN MY OWN UNSHAKABLE BELIEF. IT IS BELIEVING AN UNSHAKABLE GOD WHEN EVERY-THING IN ME TREMBLES AND QUAKES.

Praise be to You, Lord, for You showed Your wonderful love to me when I was in a besieged city (Ps. 31:21).

But Lord God, according to Your Word, these "light and momentary" troubles of mine (in relation to eternity) are achieving for me an eternal glory that far outweighs them all.

So I fix my eyes not on what is seen, but on what is unseen. For what is seen is temporary, but what is unseen is eternal (2 Cor. 4:17–18).

I am still confident of this: I will see Your goodness, Lord, in the land of the living. I will wait for You, Lord. I will be strong and take heart and wait for You (Ps. 27:13–14).

WHEN YOU REALLY LOVE SACRIFICIALLY, GOD CATCHES IT EVEN IF NO ONE ELSE DOES. IT NEVER FALLS TO THE GROUND.

Lord, according to Your Word, love is patient, love is kind. It does not envy, it does not boast, it is not proud. It is not rude, it is not self-seeking, it is not easily angered, it keeps no record of wrongs. Love does not delight in evil but rejoices with the truth. It always protects, always trusts, always hopes, always perseveres. Love never fails (I Cor. 13:4–8).

Father, I acknowledge to You that I don't begin to possess this kind of love on my own. The only way I can experience and express love like this is to surrender my heart to You, and ask You to empty it of all its fleshly contents and make it a vessel of Your love. Use my heart to love the unlovely and even those who have hurt me, dear Lord.

God has graciously allowed some of my fears to come true so I would discover I would not disintegrate.

You, Christ, were despised and rejected by men, a man of sorrows, and familiar with suffering. You were like one from whom men hide their faces. You were despised, and we did not esteem You (Isa. 53:3). You know exactly how I feel, Lord. I put my trust in You.

Mighty Redeemer, the cords of death have entangled me; the torrents of destruction have overwhelmed me. The cords of the grave have coiled around me; the snares of death have confronted me (Ps. 18:4–5).

Yet even though I walk through the valley of the shadow of death, I will fear no evil, for You are with me; Your rod and Your staff, they comfort me (Ps. 23:4).

OCTOBER

Working on our thought lives is the only thing that will keep them from working on us.

Lord, who can say, "I have kept my heart pure; I am clean and without sin?" (Prov. 20:9). I am powerless to possess a pure and clean heart on my own. Only You can do it for me.

Whatever is true, whatever is noble, whatever is right, whatever is pure, whatever is lovely, whatever is admirable—if anything is excellent or praiseworthy—help me to think about such things (Phil. 4:8–9).

Please help me, Lord, not be deceived by the serpent's cunning and allow my mind to be led astray from my new commitment of sincere and pure devotion to You (2 Cor. 11:2–3).

YOU AND I AS BELIEVERS IN
CHRIST HAVE ALSO BEEN CHOSEN
TO KNOW AND BELIEVE AND
UNDERSTAND THAT HE IS GOD.

Christ Jesus, I acknowledge that You are the ultimate mighty warrior. There is none like You! No power equals Your power! You are transcendent over all!

When I feel overwhelmed with evil all around me, help me rejoice in the vision of the apostle John, who saw heaven standing open and there before him was a white horse, whose rider is called Faithful and True.

With justice You will judge and make war. Your eyes will be like blazing fire, and on Your head will be many crowns. You have a name written on You that no one knows but You Yourself (Rev. 19:11–12).

IF SATAN CAN GET US TO DROP
OUR SHIELD OF FAITH, HE KNOWS
WE CAN'T REMAIN STANDING
FOR VERY LONG.

Help me, God, to stand firm with the belt of truth buckled around my waist, with the breastplate of righteousness in place, and with my feet fitted with the readiness that comes from the gospel of peace.

In addition to all this, help me to take up the shield of faith, with which I can extinguish all the flaming arrows of the evil one.

Help me to take the helmet of salvation and the sword of the Spirit, which is the Word of God. Help me to pray in the Spirit on all occasions with all kinds of prayers and requests. With this in mind, help me to be alert and always keep on praying for all the saints (Eph. 6:14–18).

THE CHILD OF GOD WHO TRUSTS
GOD'S LOVE POSSESSES SECURITY
IN SALVATION. WE CAN KNOW THE
FATHER WILL NOT REJECT US.

Lord, Your Word does not dwell in me if I don't believe the One You sent (John 5:38). Help me to respond to Your Son according to Your Word: "I believe and know that You are the Holy One of God" (John 6:69).

Father, please help me to examine myself to see whether I am in the faith. You instruct me to test myself and realize that Christ Jesus is in me if I have indeed received Him as Savior (2 Cor. 13:5).

Lord, though I have not seen You, I want to love You deeply; and even though I do not see You now, I want to believe in You and be filled with Your inexpressible and glorious joy (1 Pet. 1:8).

THE PEACE OF GOD SHOULD
NOT BE AN INFREQUENT
SURPRISE BUT THE ONGOING
RULE OF OUR LIVES.

Father, since I have been justified through faith, I have peace with You through my Lord Jesus Christ (Rom. 5:1).

How I praise You, my God, that in Christ and through faith in Him I may approach You with freedom and confidence! (Eph. 3:12). Help me to understand that the amount of faith I possess will greatly affect the freedom and confidence with which I approach You.

Father, You have written Your Word to those of us who believe in the name of the Son of God so that I may know I have eternal life (1 John 5:13).

Help me to know and cease doubting.

GOD DOESN'T JUST SPEAK
TO HEAR THE SOUND OF HIS
OWN VOICE. HE SPEAKS IN
ORDER TO ACCOMPLISH.

Lord, please help me to be like Abraham who, by faith, when called to go to a place he would later receive as his inheritance, obeyed and went, even though he did not know where he was going (Heb. 11:8). Help me not to miss future blessings because I refuse to go to a place with You that I've never been before.

Father, I desire to fix my eyes on Jesus, the author and perfector of my faith, who for the joy set before Him endured the cross, scorning its shame, and sat down at the right hand of the throne of God (Heb. 12:2).

Cause my faith to continue to grow, O Lord (2 Cor. 10:15).

WE'VE GOT TO WISE UP IN THE WORD
OF GOD, LEARN WHAT OUR RIGHTS
ARE, AND LEARN TO USE THE
EQUIPMENT GOD HAS GIVEN US.

I praise and magnify Your powerful name! For Your Word is living and active. Sharper than any double-edged sword, it penetrates even to dividing soul and spirit, joints and marrow; it judges the thoughts and attitudes of the heart. Nothing in all creation is hidden from Your sight. Everything is uncovered and laid bare before You (Heb. 4:12–13).

Thank You for the assurance that if I will stay in Your Word and obey Your teaching, I will quickly discern the threat of deception and will walk in truth and liberty. Your eyes see into the inmost places of my heart and mind. Help me allow You to show me things I need to see, and teach me how to be free.

How do we find the throne of grace? Follow the blood drops. The praying man is the one with bloodstains on his knees.

We all, like sheep, had gone astray, each of us had turned to his own way; but the Lord laid on You, Jesus, the iniquity of us all (Isa. 53:3–6). O Lord, because You are my help, I sing in the shadow of Your wings. My soul clings to You; Your right hand upholds me (Ps. 63:7–8).

When Your kindness and love appeared, You saved me, not because of righteous things I had done, but because of Your mercy. You saved me through the washing of rebirth and renewal by the Holy Spirit, whom You poured out on me generously through Jesus Christ my Savior, so that, having been justified by Your grace, I would become an heir having the hope of eternal life (Titus 3:4–7).

IF YOU'VE BEEN REJECTED BY SOME-ONE YOU LOVE, YOU'LL AGREE FEW INJURIES ARE MORE EXCRUCIATING. BUT GOD WILL NOT FORSAKE YOU.

Merciful, compassionate God, even my close friend, whom I trusted, he who shared my bread, has lifted up his heel against me. But Lord, have mercy on me; raise me up.

Empower me to live a life pleasing to You, and my enemy will not be able to triumph over me. Lord, as a New Testament believer, uphold me in Your integrity instead of my own and set me in Your presence forever (Ps. 41:9–12).

One of us can rout a thousand, because You, the Lord our God, fights for us, just as You promised. Faithful God, help me to be very careful to love You, the Lord my God (Josh. 23:10–11).

ANY SACRIFICE WE MAKE IN OUR QUEST FOR FREEDOM WILL BE WHOLLY CONSUMED AND BLESSED BY GOD.

Father, You urge me in Your absolute mercy toward me to offer my body as a living sacrifice, holy and pleasing to God. This is my spiritual act of worship.

You call on me not to conform any longer to the pattern of this world, but to be transformed by the renewing of my mind. Then I will be able to test and approve what Your will is—Your good, pleasing, and perfect will! (Rom. 12:1–2).

Father, help me to clothe myself with the Lord Jesus Christ and not to think about how to gratify the desires of the sinful nature (Rom. 13:14). I desperately need Your help to do this, Father! Teach me and help me!

God has a will for your life, Christ has a word for your life, and the Holy Spirit has a way for your life.

Lord God, Your Word says that I was once alienated from God and was an enemy in my mind because of my evil behavior. But now You have reconciled me by Christ's physical body through death to present me holy in Your sight, without blemish and free from accusation (Col. 1:21–22). O Lord, how I celebrate being free from accusation!

I thank You that my citizenship is in heaven. I eagerly await a Savior from there, the Lord Jesus Christ, who, by the power that enables Him to bring everything under His control, will transform my lowly body so that it will be like His glorious body (Phil. 3:20–21). How I celebrate the fact that You have power to bring everything under Your control!

HUMBLING OURSELVES DOESN'T
MEAN HATING OURSELVES. HUMILITY
CAN BE RATHER EASILY ATTAINED BY
JUST OPENING OUR EYES TO REALITY.

Lord, help me to be very careful not to think of myself more highly than I ought, but rather think of myself with sober judgment, in accordance with the measure of faith God has given me (Rom. 12:3).

Help me also not to think of myself as anything less than a child of Yours, God, dearly loved by You (Eph. 5:1). Your deep desire is for me to possess both humility and security.

God, I am so thankful there is now no condemnation for those who are in Christ Jesus (Rom. 8:1). If You do not condemn me, I have no right or place to condemn myself. Help me not to get caught up in a defeating cycle of self-condemnation.

CAN YOU THINK OF A TIME WHEN
YOU WERE SUDDENLY AWASH WITH
THE MAGNITUDE OF GOD'S LOVE
FOR YOU PERSONALLY?

Lord God, like Your people Israel, You will ransom me from the hand of those stronger than me. I will come and shout for joy on the heights of Zion; I will rejoice in the bounty of the Lord—the grain, the new wine and the oil, the young of the flocks and herds. I will be like a well-watered garden and I will sorrow no more. I will dance and be glad.

You will turn my mourning into gladness; You will give me comfort and joy instead of sorrow. You have declared that You will satisfy Your people with abundance, and we will be filled with Your bounty (Jer. 31:11–14).

Lord, You will refresh the weary and the faint (Jer. 31:25).

NONE OF US REACH ADULTHOOD WITHOUT SOME HOLES IN OUR LIVES. SOME HAVE MORE THAN OTHERS, BUT WE ALL HAVE HOLES.

Help me, Lord, to finally comprehend what it means to consider it pure joy whenever I face trials of many kinds. Help me to know that the testing of my faith develops perseverance. And perseverance must finish its work in me so that I may be mature and complete, lacking nothing (James 1:2–4).

Lord, You are not asking me to rejoice that I have lost someone or something precious, but You know that in my loss I can rejoice in all I have to gain if I'm willing. Never must my suffering be in vain.

Merciful Lord, restore to me the joy of Your salvation and grant me a willing spirit, to sustain me (Ps. 51:12).

He delights in
nothing more than our
choice to believe him over
what we see and feel.

Lord God, I know that when the earthly tents we live in are destroyed, we who are believers have a building from You, an eternal house in heaven, not built by human hands.

Meanwhile I groan, longing to be clothed with my heavenly dwelling. For while in this tent, I groan and am burdened, because I do not wish to be unclothed but clothed with my heavenly dwelling, so that what is mortal may be swallowed up by life.

Now it is You, God, who have made me for this very purpose and have given me the Spirit as a deposit, guaranteeing what is to come (2 Cor. 5:1–5). Help me to be confident in the reality of heaven.

BEFORE WE CAN EVEN BEGIN TO GIVE GOD'S LOVE AWAY, WE'VE GOT TO FULLY ACCEPT IT AND ITS POWER FOR OURSELVES.

Lord, I have the treasure of Your Holy Spirit in me, a simple jar of clay, to show that this all-surpassing power is from God and not from me (2 Cor. 4:7). Lord, forgiving someone who has hurt me deeply is sometimes the way the power of the Holy Spirit is made most conspicuous in me. Forgive through me, Jesus. I am powerless without You. Show what You can do through my vessel. I offer myself to You for this authentic God-work.

Not by might nor by power, but by Your Spirit, Lord Almighty (Zech. 4:6), I will be able to forgive. Your Word assures me that it is You who works in me to will and to act according to Your good purpose (Phil. 2:13).

WILL YOU CONTINUE TO SIT IN A DARK TOMB, OR WILL YOU WALK INTO THE LIGHT OF RESURRECTION LIFE? LAZARUS, COME FORTH!

Your eyes, Lord, are on those who fear You, on those whose hope is in Your unfailing love, to deliver them from death and keep them alive in famine.

I wait in hope for You, Lord; You are my help and my shield. In You my heart rejoices, for I trust in Your holy name. May Your unfailing love rest upon me, O Lord, even as I put my hope in You (Ps. 33:18–22).

As for me, O God, I will always have hope; I will praise You more and more (Ps. 71:14). May those who fear You rejoice when they see me, for I have put my hope in Your Word (Ps. 119:74). You, Lord, delight in those who fear You, who put their hope in Your unfailing love (Ps. 147:11).

GOD WILL GIVE US VICTORY,
BUT SOMETIMES HE WILL REQUIRE
EVERY OUNCE OF ENERGY AND COOP-
ERATION WE HAVE IN THE PROCESS.

Blessed, merciful God, Your Word promises that those who sow in tears will reap with songs of joy. If I go out weeping, carrying seed to sow, I will return with songs of joy, carrying sheaves with me (Ps. 126:5–6).

Help me to see that the promise is not made to those who simply have tears but to those who are willing to sow seed in the midst of their tears. Your Word tells us in Luke 8:11 that the seed is the Word. If I'm willing to keep believing and sowing Your Word, even when I am desperately hurting, You will bring me forth from this difficult season with songs of joy. Because of Your faithfulness, with joy I will draw water from the wells of salvation (Isa. 12:3).

FINDING SATISFACTION AND
FULLNESS IN CHRIST WAS NEVER
MEANT TO BE A SECRET TREASURE
THAT ONLY A FEW COULD FIND.

Father God, help me to recognize and understand how Satan's role as accuser of believers affects me. Your Word says he accuses Christians day and night (Rev. 12:10). Please help me to discern the difference between true conviction of sin from the Holy Spirit and wrongful accusation from the kingdom of darkness.

I thank You that because I am in Christ, Satan, the prince of this world, has no hold on me (John 14:30). Father, Your Word tells me that the accuser of believers is overcome by the blood of the Lamb and by the word of our testimony (Rev. 12:11). Help me to use the power You have given me to overcome the enemy when he wars against me.

KNOWING AND CLAIMING GOD'S WORD WHEN ATTACKED BLOWS THE HEAD OFF ENEMY FORCES.

Father God, help me to remember how Your Son responded when tempted by the devil when He was in the wilderness. He responded to Him with Your Word! (Matt. 4:1–11). Help me to hide Your Word in my heart (Ps. 119:11), so that I am ready to resist when the enemy taunts me with temptation.

Lord, if You ever give Satan permission to sift me as wheat, I earnestly pray to be faithful to You and to emerge from the difficult season with a fresh ability to strengthen my brothers and sisters in Christ (Luke 22:31).

My Father, please help me to be on my guard; stand firm in the faith; be a person of courage; be strong; and to do everything in love (1 Cor. 16:13).

ANY KIND OF DEATH IS AN
INVITATION TO RESURRECTION
LIFE FOR A BELIEVER. OUR SAVIOR IS
THE GOD OF RESURRECTION LIFE.

Praise be to You, my God and the Father of my Lord Jesus Christ! In Your great mercy You have given me new birth into a living hope through the resurrection of Jesus Christ from the dead, and into an inheritance that can never perish, spoil, or fade—kept in heaven for me, who through faith is shielded by God's power (1 Pet. 1:3–5).

Father, Your Word emphatically states that You do not lie. You promised before the beginning of time that faith and knowledge rest on the hope of eternal life (Titus 1:2).

Lord, You are so trustworthy. You have given me eternal life. Please grow me in the faith and knowledge that rests upon it.

THE DEEPER YOU AND I ARE ROOTED IN THE UNFAILING LOVE OF GOD, THE LESS WE SWAY WHEN THE WINDS OF LIFE BLOW HARSHLY.

Father, You have warned me for my own good not to trust anything about my heart unless it is fully surrendered to You. My heart is deceitful above all things and beyond cure. I will never be able to understand it. You the Lord search the heart and examine the mind (Jer. 17:9–10).

Please help me to recognize that the primary target of deception is my heart. In other words, I must be careful not to trust feelings and emotions on their own. I must wear the breastplate of righteousness so that I will do the right thing even when I don't feel the right thing. In the meantime, I ask You, Lord, to knead the right kind of feelings into my heart.

GOD DESIRES TO PERMEATE EVERY
INCH OF YOUR LIFE AND FILL UP
EVERY HOLLOW PLACE WITH THE
FULLNESS OF HIS LOVE.

Lord God, according to Your Word, You set apart Your children from the nations to be Your own (Lev. 20:26). Your Word tells me to know assuredly that You, the Lord, have set apart the godly for Yourself; You, Lord, will hear when I call to You (Ps. 4:3).

Help me to see and believe that You, the Sovereign Lord, come with power, and Your arm rules for You. Your reward is with You, and Your recompense accompanies You. You tend Your flock like a shepherd: You gather the lambs in Your arms and carry them close to Your heart; You gently lead those that have young (Isa. 40:10–11).

O Lord, help me to realize that You love me and care so deeply for me!

ONLY THE PLACES WHERE WE ALLOW THE LOVE OF GOD TO FULLY PENETRATE WILL BE SATISFIED AND THEREFORE LIBERATED.

God, I pray that out of Your glorious riches You will strengthen me with power through Your Spirit in my inner being, so that Christ may dwell in my heart through faith. And I pray that I, being rooted and established in love, may have power, together with all the saints, to grasp how wide and long and high and deep is the love of Christ, and to know this love that surpasses knowledge—that I may be filled to the measure of all the fullness of God. Now to You who are able to do immeasurably more than all I ask or imagine, according to Your power that is at work within me, to You be glory in the church and in Christ Jesus throughout all generations, for ever and ever! Amen (Eph. 3:16–21).

IF HE HAS BECOME GOD ALONE TO
YOU, GIVING POWERFUL EVIDENCE
OF HIS UNFAILING LOVE, YOU HAVE
A STORY TO TELL. START TALKING.

You are the Lord my God, who brought me out of slavery; You broke the bars of my yoke and enabled me to walk with my head held high (Lev. 26:13). How I thank You for this, O Lord!

For surely, Lord, You bless the righteous; You surround them with Your favor as with a shield (Ps. 5:12).

O Father, please help me to be Your idea of righteous. I know that on my own, my righteousness is as filthy rags before You, but because I have received Christ and daily desire to walk with Him, I now stand in His righteousness. Help me to flesh out His righteousness in my life.

GOD'S WILLINGNESS AND
UNWAVERING DESIRE TO BLESS HIS
PEOPLE IS ONE OF THE MOST
REPETITIVE CONCEPTS IN HIS WORD.

Lord, I believe that Your heart toward
Your children today is like Your heart toward
the children of Israel. I believe You also took
us from the ends of the earth; from its farthest
corners You called us. You said, "You are my
servants; I have chosen you and have not rejected you. So do not fear, for I am with you;
do not be dismayed, for I am your God. I will
strengthen you and help you; I will uphold you
with my righteous right hand."

One day because of You, I will search for
my enemies and will not find them. Those who
wage war against me will be as nothing at all.
For You are the Lord, my God, who takes hold
of my right hand and says to me, "Do not fear;
I will help you" (Isa. 41:9–13).

WE CAN DO ALL THINGS THROUGH
CHRIST WHO STRENGTHENS US,
BUT FRANKLY WE WON'T IF WE'RE
TOO AFRAID TO TRY.

My mighty God, thank You for Your Word that exhorts me not to become weary in doing good. At the proper time I will reap a harvest if I do not give up (Gal. 6:9).

Father, this process of breaking free is hard work! Please remind me often that it is also a very good work. Help me to know without a doubt that any effort You require of me will have effect. Please help me never to give up, no matter how long it takes. I will reap a harvest, in Jesus' name!

Lord God, I acknowledge the promise of Your Word that I can do everything through Christ who gives me strength (Phil. 4:13). Help me to cast all my anxiety on You because You care for me (1 Pet. 5:7).

WHILE SALVATION COMES AS A GIFT
OF GOD, WE FIND SATISFACTION IN
HIM AS WE DELIBERATELY SURRENDER
ALL PARTS OF OUR LIVES TO HIM.

Father, according to Your Word, at one time I was separate from Christ, excluded from citizenship in Israel and foreigner to the covenants of the promise, without hope and without God in the world. But now in Christ Jesus I who once was far away have been brought near through the blood of Christ (Eph. 2:12–13). O Lord, help me to sense Your nearness!

Awesome God, Your Word says that knowing Christ Jesus my Lord is so wonderful that I can consider everything a loss compared to its surpassing greatness. Help me to consider anything rubbish that I have to lay down in order to gain more knowledge and a more abiding presence of Christ (Phil. 3:8).

IF WE ARE NOT OCCUPIED BY THE HOLY SPIRIT, WE HAVE NOTHING OF GOD IN US FOR HIM TO SHOW.

Lord, the fruit of Your Spirit is love, joy, peace, patience, kindness, goodness, faithfulness, gentleness, and self-control. Against such things there is no law (Gal. 5:22–23). Please fill me with Your Spirit and eclipse my personality with Yours.

Lord, whatever is true, whatever is noble, whatever is right, whatever is pure, whatever is lovely, whatever is admirable—if anything is excellent or praiseworthy—help me to make the choice to think about such things (Phil. 4:8). Lord God, help me to feed the Spirit, not the flesh! Changing the way I think will change the way I feel!

Love is not only something God does, love is something He is. God would have to stop being in order to stop loving.

Wonderful Savior, Jesus, how I thank You for telling us that there will be more rejoicing in heaven over one sinner who repents than over ninety-nine righteous persons who do not need to repent (Luke 15:7).

Lord Jesus, I don't need to let my heart be troubled. I can trust in God, and I can trust also in You.

In the Father's house are many rooms; if it were not so, You would have told me. You went to prepare a place for us. And if You went to prepare a place for us, You will come back and take us to be with You that we also may be where You are (John 14:1–3).

THE MOST WONDERFUL ASSURANCE
OF GOD'S PRESENCE IS PROBABLY
WITHIN YOUR REACH AT THIS VERY
MOMENT——HIS WORD!

I can do all things through You, Jesus, who gives me strength (Phil. 4:13).

What You are commanding me is not too difficult for me or beyond my reach. It is not up in heaven, so that I have to ask, "Who will ascend into heaven to get it and proclaim it to me so I may obey it?" Nor is it beyond the sea, so that I have to ask, "Who will cross the sea to get it and proclaim it to me so I may obey it?" No, the Word is very near me; it is in my mouth and in my heart so I may obey it (Deut. 30:11–14).

I humble myself, therefore, under Your mighty hand, God, that You may lift me up in due time. I cast all this anxiety on You because You care for me (1 Pet. 5:6–7).

NOVEMBER

THE WORD OF GOD IS ONLY ALIVE, EFFECTIVE, AND POWERFUL IN US WHEN WE RECEIVE IT.

Your precepts, O Lord, are right, giving joy to the heart. Your commands are radiant, giving light to my eyes (Ps. 19:8).

O God, speak to me so clearly through Your Word that I recognize Your voice. Help me to understand what You are making known to me, delighting me with Your Word so that I may celebrate with great joy! (Neh. 8:12).

If Your law had not been my delight, I would have perished in my affliction (Ps. 119:92). Teach me Your Word during this season of my life like I have never known it before, and make this verse my testimony when I emerge from this place.

WE WERE CREATED FOR THE PURPOSE OF GIVING CHRIST'S INVISIBLE CHARACTER A GLIMPSE OF VISIBILITY.

Lord, many have run this difficult race faithfully. I want to be among them. Therefore, since I am surrounded by such a great cloud of witnesses, help me throw off everything that hinders and the sin that so easily entangles, and help me run with perseverance the race marked out for me.

Help me fix my eyes on You, Jesus, the author and perfecter of my faith, who for the joy set before You endured the cross, scorning its shame, and sat down at the right hand of the throne of God (Heb. 12:1–2).

As a bridegroom rejoices over his bride, so will You, my God, rejoice over me at Your appearing (Isa. 62:5).

GOD WOULD RATHER HEAR OUR
HONEST PLEAS FOR MORE OF WHAT
WE LACK THAN PIOUS PLATITUDES
FROM AN UNBELIEVING HEART.

Create in me a pure heart, O God, and renew a steadfast spirit within me. . . . Restore to me the joy of Your salvation and grant me a willing spirit to sustain me (Ps. 51:10, 12).

Help me to rid myself of all malice and all deceit, hypocrisy, envy, and slander of every kind. Like a newborn baby, help me to crave pure spiritual milk, so that by it I may grow up in my salvation, now that I have tasted that the Lord is good (1 Pet. 2:1–2).

Lord, Your Word says how I can keep my way pure: by living according to Your Word. I will seek You with all my heart; help me not to stray from Your commands. Help me to hide Your Word in my heart that I might not sin against You (Ps. 119:9–11).

EVERY TIME WE SUFFER LOSS, WE HAVE AN OPPORTUNITY FOR THE LOSS TO BRING GAIN FOR JESUS' SAKE BY ALLOWING HIS LIFE TO BE REVEALED.

I pray to You, O Lord, in the time of Your favor; in Your great love, O God, answer me with Your sure salvation.

Rescue me from the mire, do not let me sink; deliver me from those who hate me, from the deep waters. Do not let the floodwaters engulf me or the depths swallow me up or the pit close its mouth over me.

Answer me, O Lord, out of the goodness of Your love; in Your great mercy turn to me. Do not hide Your face from Your servant; answer me quickly, for I am in trouble (Ps. 69:13–17).

According to Your Word, in this world I will have trouble, but I am to take heart! You have overcome the world! (John 16:33).

DON'T THINK FOR A MOMENT THAT SATAN IS GOING TO SLOW DOWN WHEN HE SEES YOU IN THE WAY.

Lord God, Your Word tells me that I must be self-controlled and alert. My enemy the devil prowls around like a roaring lion looking for someone to devour. Please empower me to resist him, standing firm in the faith, because I can know my brothers and sisters throughout the world are undergoing the same kind of sufferings (1 Pet. 5:8–9).

How I praise You that the reason the Son of God appeared was to destroy the devil's work. No one who is born of God will continue to sin, because God's seed remains in him; he cannot go on sinning, because he has been born of God (1 John 3:8–9).

Please lead me not into temptation but deliver me from the evil one (Matt. 6:13).

WE CAN READ SCRIPTURE FOR
HOURS, BUT IF WE DON'T RECEIVE IT
BY FAITH, IT DOESN'T ABIDE IN US,
BRINGING ITS VITALITY AND ENERGY.

Father, by faith in the name of Jesus, make me strong. Help me to realize that it is Jesus' name and the faith that comes through Him that heal me (Acts 3:16).

Father God, the messages I hear from Your Word will have no value to me if I do not combine them with faith (Heb. 4:2). Help me to combine each message I hear from Your Word with faith; then great value will result.

According to Your Word, faith is being sure of what I hope for and certain of what I do not see (Heb. 11:1). Please increase my assurance and certainty of the things You've promised but that I cannot see.

We are incapable of loving others in Jesus' name for nothing, loving them for the sake of his sacrificial legacy.

Christ Jesus, in You neither circumcision nor uncircumcision has any value. The only thing that counts is faith expressing itself through love (Gal. 5:6).

O God, let it be said of me that my faith is growing more and more, and the love I have for others is increasing! (2 Thess. 1:3). How I pray that You may count me worthy of Your calling, and that by Your power You may fulfill every good purpose of mine and every act prompted by my faith (2 Thess. 1:11).

Lord God, I desire that these things will be remembered before You: my work produced by faith, my labor prompted by love, and my endurance inspired by hope in my Lord Jesus Christ (1 Thess. 1:3).

How many weary people do we encounter day after day who could use a sustaining word?

Lord, You look down upon the masses of people on this earth and have compassion on them. So many are harassed and helpless, like sheep without a shepherd (Matt. 9:36).

Put Your words in my mouth and cover me with the shadow of Your hand—You who set the heavens in place, who laid the foundations of the earth, and who say to Your children, "You are my people" (Isa. 51:16).

Father, help me to encourage others daily, as long as it is called "today," so that they may not be hardened by sin's deceitfulness (Heb. 3:13). Send me encouragers when I need them as well. Your Word clearly teaches that sin's deceitfulness hardens us. Keep me tender through Your truth.

WHEN OUR HEARTS ARE HEMORRHAGING, NEVER FORGET THAT CHRIST BINDS AND COMPRESSES THEM WITH A NAIL-SCARRED HAND.

Father, I thank You for the vivid picture You paint in Your Word as You promise to cover me with Your feathers and grant me refuge under Your wings; Your faithfulness will be my shield and rampart.

I need not fear the terror of night, nor the arrow that flies by day, nor the pestilence that stalks in the darkness, nor the plague that destroys at midday. A thousand may fall at my side, ten thousand at my right hand, but You will keep destruction from coming near me (Ps. 91:4–7).

You, Lord God, are with me, You are mighty to save. You will take great delight in me, You will quiet me with Your love, You will rejoice over me with singing! (Zeph. 3:17).

THE MOST EFFECTIVE KEY TO BELIEVING GOD IS RIGHT BEFORE OUR EYES. THE MORE WE KNOW HIM, THE MORE WE WILL BELIEVE HIM.

My faithful God, I thank You for the grace, mercy, and peace from You the Father and from Jesus Christ, Your Son, that is with me in truth and love (2 John 3).

Help me to know the grace of my Lord Jesus Christ, that though He was rich, yet for my sake He became poor, so that I through His poverty might become rich (2 Cor. 8:9). Please help me to continually discover the riches of Christ in my life, Lord.

Lord God, You have chosen those who are poor in the eyes of the world to be rich in faith and to inherit the kingdom You promised those who love You (James 2:5). Cause me to be rich in faith, Lord!

MAY GOD REMIND US DAILY THAT
WE ARE LOVED AND EMPOWERED
BY THE ONE WHO BROUGHT THE
UNIVERSE INTO EXISTENCE.

Father God, Your Word says for everyone who is godly to pray to You while You may be found; surely when the mighty waters rise, they will not reach me.

You are my hiding place; You will protect me from trouble and surround me with songs of deliverance (Ps. 32:6–7). O thank You, God!

According to Your Word, those who put their trust in You are like Mount Zion, which cannot be shaken but endures forever. As the mountains surround Jerusalem, so the Lord surrounds His people both now and forevermore (Ps. 125:1–2).

Hallelujah!

ALTHOUGH WE NEED TO BE SAVED
FROM ETERNAL SEPARATION ONLY
ONCE, CHRIST CONTINUES HIS SAVING
WORK IN US THE REST OF OUR LIVES.

Lord, please help me not to be like Ephraim whom You taught to walk, taking them by the arms; but they did not realize it was You who healed them. Please help me to realize without a doubt that You are the One who heals me.

Like Ephraim, You have led me with cords of human kindness, with ties of love; You lifted the yoke from my neck and bent down to feed me (Hos. 11:3–4). Help me to acknowledge You daily and never forget who teaches me how to walk.

I acknowledge that it is by grace I have been saved, through faith—and this not from myself; it is the gift of God (Eph. 2:8).

IT IS IN OUR WEAKNESS THAT HE
IS STRONG. IT IS AS WE BEND THE
KNEE TO HIS LORDSHIP THAT GOD
IS ABLE TO DELIVER US.

You are my lamp, O Lord; the Lord turns my darkness into light. With Your help I can advance against a troop; with my God I can scale a wall.

As for You, my God, Your way is perfect; the word of the Lord is flawless. You are a shield for all who take refuge in You. For who is God besides You, Lord? And who is the Rock except my God?

It is You, God, who arms me with strength and makes my way perfect. You make my feet like the feet of a deer; You enable me to stand on the heights. You train my hands for battle; my arms can bend a bow of bronze. You give me Your shield of victory; You stoop down to make me great (2 Sam. 22:29–36).

BELIEVE EVEN WHEN YOU DO NOT
FEEL. KNOW EVEN WHEN YOU DO NOT
SEE. HE GAVE THE LIFE OF HIS SON TO
DEMONSTRATE HIS LOVE. BELIEVE!

Lord God, Your Word says that You love the just and will not forsake Your faithful ones. They will be protected forever (Ps. 37:28). My justification is found in Your Son, my Savior, Jesus Christ (Rom. 8:30). He is faithful even when I am not (2 Tim. 2:13). Thank You, Father, that I can be absolutely sure You will never leave me or forsake me, because I am in Jesus (Heb. 13:5).

O God, how I thank You that a lack of faith will never nullify Your faithfulness (Rom. 3:3). If I am faithless, You will remain faithful, for You cannot disown Yourself (2 Tim. 2:13). Lord, help me to know that I belong to the truth, and set my heart at rest in Your presence (1 John 3:19).

COMPLETELY SURRENDER YOUR HURT TO HIM, WITHHOLDING NOTHING, AND INVITE HIM TO WORK MIRACLES FROM YOUR MISERY.

Lord God, I am hard pressed on every side, but not crushed; perplexed, but not in despair; persecuted, but not abandoned; struck down, but not destroyed. I always carry around in my body the death of Your Son, Jesus, so that the life of Jesus may also be revealed in my mortal body (2 Cor. 4:8–10).

Help me always to remember that if I am truly crucified with Christ, I am also raised to resurrection life! Help me never to forget that the purpose of crucified life is to walk in the power of Your resurrection (Gal. 2:20).

Thank You for raising me up with Christ and seating me with Him in the heavenly realms in Christ Jesus! (Eph. 2:6).

PERHAPS THE MOST PROFOUND
MIRACLE OF ALL IS LIVING
THROUGH SOMETHING WE
THOUGHT WOULD KILL US.

I pray that out of Your glorious riches You will strengthen me with power through Your Spirit in my inner being, so that Christ may dwell in my heart through faith.

And I pray that I, being rooted and established in love, may have power, together with all the saints, to grasp how wide and long and high and deep is the love of Christ, and to know this love that surpasses knowledge—that I may be filled to the measure of all the fullness of God (Eph. 3:16–19).

Father, help me to be confident of this, that He who began a good work in me will carry it on to completion until the day of Christ Jesus (Phil. 1:6).

GOD NEVER MEANT FOR US TO SIP
HIS SPIRIT LIKE A PROPER CUP OF TEA.
HE MEANT FOR US TO LAP UP HIS LIFE
WITH UNQUENCHABLE THIRST.

Lord, I know what it is to be in need, and I know what it is to have plenty. I want to learn the secret of being content in any and every situation, whether well fed or hungry, whether living in plenty or in want. I can do everything through You, Lord, who gives me strength (Phil. 4:12–13).

Lord, You beckon me in Your Word to come to You when I'm thirsty, to come to the waters; I can come to You when I have no money. I can come, buy, and eat! Why do I spend money and labor on things that don't satisfy? Your Word tells me to listen to You and eat what is good, and my soul will delight in the richest of fare (Isa. 55:1–2).

WHEN WE PRAY THE SCRIPTURE,
WE TRANSFER THE BURDEN TO GOD'S
WORD RATHER THAN OUR ABILITY TO
PRAY CORRECTLY OR ADEQUATELY.

Lord God, Your Holy Spirit helps me in my weakness. I do not know what I ought to pray for, but the Spirit Himself intercedes for me with groans that words cannot express. And He who searches my heart knows the mind of the Spirit, because Your Spirit intercedes for me in accordance with Your will (Rom. 8:26–27).

Help me, then, Lord, not to be anxious about anything, but in everything, by prayer and petition, with thanksgiving, present my requests to You. And Your peace, which transcends all understanding, will guard my heart and my mind in Christ Jesus (Phil. 4:6–7).

Christ never allows the hearts of his own to be shattered without excellent reasons and eternal purposes.

Glorious Lord God, one day I will hear a loud voice from Your throne saying, "Now the dwelling of God is with men, and he will live with them." We will be Your people, and You Yourself will be with us and be our God.

You will wipe away every tear from our eyes. There will be no more death or mourning or crying or pain, for the old order of things will pass away. You who are seated on the throne will say, "I am making everything new!" These words are trustworthy and true! (Rev. 21:3–5).

Lord God, help me presently believe, then one day see, that my present sufferings cannot be compared to the glory that You will reveal in me (Rom. 8:18).

NO MATTER HOW LONG WE'VE
WALKED WITH GOD, WE WILL STILL
HAVE DAYS THAT SEEM DARK. IN
THOSE TIMES, RELY ON WHO HE IS.

Faithful and merciful God, You have set my iniquities before You, my secret sins in the light of Your presence (Ps. 90:8). Help me not be afraid of letting You all the way into the secret places of my heart and mind . . . for You, Lord, are already there!

Your Word is a lamp to my feet and a light for my path (Ps. 119:105). Please help me to take this verse literally, Lord. Your Word will bring light to me during this dark season. Satan wants me to resist the very thing I need the most. Woo me to Your Word, O God!

Send forth Your light and Your truth, Lord, let them guide me; let them bring me to Your holy mountain, to the place where You dwell (Ps. 43:3).

GOD DOES NOT LOVE US LESS WHEN
HE GIVES US FEWER EVIDENCES.
HE SIMPLY DESIRES TO GROW US UP
AND TEACH US TO WALK BY FAITH.

Lord, according to Your Word, hope deferred makes the heart sick, but a longing fulfilled is a tree of life (Prov. 13:12). Lord, You are keenly aware of any hopes that have been deferred in my life. Help me to put my hopes in You, for You will fulfill my longings.

Wonderful Savior, You tell me that there is surely a future hope for me, and my hope will not be cut off (Prov. 23:18). When I hope in You, Lord, I will renew my strength. I will soar on wings like eagles; I will run and not grow weary, I will walk and not be faint (Isa. 40:31).

Lord, help me hear this word as one from You to me: "So there is hope for your future," declares the Lord (Jer. 29:17).

Hoping we're on the right track will never dig a deep enough path to follow to our promised lands.

Lord of glory, You have a plan for me that no eye has seen, no ear has heard, and no mind has conceived. Your gracious Holy Spirit reveals this awesome plan to those who love You (1 Cor. 2:9).

I acknowledge that Satan's ploy is to keep me from fulfilling Your plan for my life. Please help me to resist him and overcome his assaults on my life. I want to do Your will, O God.

Lord, help me to keep my eyes looking straight ahead and fix my gaze directly before me. Make level paths for my feet and strengthen me to take only the ways that are firm. Help me not to swerve to the right or the left; keep my feet from evil (Prov. 4:25–27).

Bending the knee is ultimately a matter of obedience. Obedience is always the mark of authentic surrender to God's authority.

Father God, You said of Your children long ago, "If my people would but listen to me, if Israel would follow my ways, how quickly would I subdue their enemies and turn my hand against their foes!" (Ps. 81:13–14).

Please help me to listen carefully to You and follow Your ways so that I will not hinder my own victory through disobedience.

Father, Your Word says that I, Your child, was called to be free. Please help me not to use my freedom to indulge the sinful nature; rather, help me to use my freedom to serve others in love (Gal. 5:13). Help me, Lord, to take Your yoke upon me and learn from You, for You are gentle and humble in heart, and I will find rest for my soul (Matt. 11:29).

IF GOD HAS ALLOWED SOMETHING
DIFFICULT TO HAPPEN TO ONE OF
HIS CHILDREN, HE PLANS TO USE IT
MIGHTILY, IF THE CHILD LETS HIM.

God, You have ascended amid shouts of joy, the Lord amid the sounding of trumpets. For You, Lord God, are the King of all the earth; I will sing to You a psalm of praise (Ps. 47:5–7).

Praise You, my God! Let the sound of Your praise be heard; You have preserved my life and kept my feet from slipping. For You, O God, tested me; You refined me like silver (Ps. 66:8–10).

May You arise, God, may Your enemies be scattered; may Your foes flee before You. I desire to sing to You, O God, and sing praises in Your name. I extol You who rides on the clouds—Your name is the Lord. I rejoice before You! (Ps. 68:1, 4).

THE ONE WHO CUT COVENANT WITH
US THROUGH THE TORN BLOOD OF
JESUS IS THE SAME ONE WHO SITS
UPON THE UNIVERSE'S THRONE.

You, Lord, reign! You are robed in majesty
and are armed with strength! Your throne was
established long ago: You are from all eternity.
You are mightier than the thunder of the great
waters, mightier than the breakers of the sea—
the Lord on high is mighty! (Ps. 93:1–2, 4).

The Lord reigns; let the earth be glad; let
the distant shores rejoice. Fire goes before You,
Lord, and consumes Your foes on every side.
Your lightning lights up the world; the earth
sees and trembles. The mountains melt like
wax before You, Lord. The heavens proclaim
Your righteousness and all the people see Your
glory (Ps. 97:1, 3–6).

NONE OF US CONSISTENTLY GLORIFY GOD IN EVERYTHING WE SAY AND DO, BUT WE CAN STILL EXPERIENCE GENUINE LIBERATION IN CHRIST.

You, the Lord my God, are my sun and shield; You, Lord, bestow favor and honor; no good thing do You withhold from those whose walk is blameless (Ps. 84:11).

Lord, I can't claim a blameless walk, but I ask You to please empower me to walk with You faithfully and to never cease pursuing it. Help me, Lord, to hold unswervingly to the hope I profess, for You who promised are faithful (Heb. 10:23).

If I do away with the yoke of oppression, with the pointing finger and malicious talk, and if I spend myself in behalf of the hungry and satisfy the needs of the oppressed, then light will rise in the darkness, and my night will become like noonday (Isa. 58:9–10).

GOD HAS A ONE-TRACK MIND
AS FAR AS WE ARE CONCERNED.
HE WANTS US TO LIVE LIKE THE
OVERCOMERS WE ARE.

Father, Your Word exhorts me to set my mind on things above, not on earthly things (Col. 3:2). This can be such a battle, Lord! Please help me every single day to set my mind on You.

I am always confident and know that as long as I am at home in the body I am away from the Lord. I live by faith, not by sight.

I am confident, I say, and would prefer to be away from the body and at home with You, Lord. So I make it my goal to please You, whether I am at home in the body or away from it (2 Cor. 5:6–9).

Until then, help me to allow You to live through me so that I might be faithful.

WHY ARE WE SO SAFE IN THE THINGS WE PRAY? WHO ARE WE TRYING TO KEEP FROM LOOKING FOOLISH? US OR HIM?

God, for now I know in part and I prophesy in part, but when perfection comes, the imperfect disappears. When I was a child, I talked like a child, I thought like a child, I reasoned like a child. I now desire to put my childish ways behind me.

Now I see but a poor reflection as in a mirror; then I will see face-to-face. Now I know in part; then I shall know fully, Lord, even as I am fully known. And now these three remain: faith, hope, and love. But the greatest of these is love (1 Cor. 13:9–13).

Help me prioritize the things that will always remain. Faith lives in all the places I wait to know fully.

IT IS FOR FREEDOM CHRIST HAS SET
US FREE. THE QUESTION IS WHETHER
OR NOT WE ARE READY TO PREPARE
THE WAY FOR OUR LIBERATOR.

Lord God, You teach me that man does not live on bread alone but on every word that comes from the mouth of the Lord (Deut. 8:3). Please develop in me a hunger for Your presence and Your Word that exceeds any physical cravings I could ever experience.

Your Word tells me that one handful with tranquility is better than two handfuls with toil and chasing after the wind (Eccles. 4:6). Please set me free from the false security that comes from having more of anything than I really need.

Help me to know Your love that surpasses knowledge—that I may be filled to the measure of all the fullness of God (Eph. 3:19).

Expose your heart one more time . . . just to Jesus. After all, this is what his Father sent him to do.

Lord, according to Your Word, what a man desires or craves deeply is unfailing love (Prov. 19:22). Every other use of the words "unfailing love" in Scripture is attributed to You alone. You are the only one capable of perpetually unfailing love. Help me to understand that my deep cravings for someone to love me with that kind of love were meant to be satisfied in You alone.

Lord God, in Your love You kept me from the pit of destruction; You have put all my sins behind Your back (Isa. 38:17). You will never fail to forgive the truly repentant sinner, O Lord, because You love us so much, You want us to have the full measure of Your joy within us (John 17:13).

DECEMBER

PEACE CAN BE POSSIBLE IN ANY
SITUATION, BUT WE CANNOT
PRODUCE IT ON DEMAND. IT IS
A FRUIT OF THE SPIRIT.

God of hope, please fill me with all joy and peace as I trust in You, so that I may overflow with hope by the power of the Holy Spirit (Rom. 15:13). Let me hear joy and gladness; let the bones You have crushed rejoice (Ps. 51:8).

O God, those living far away fear Your wonders; where morning dawns and evening fades You call forth songs of joy.... The meadows are covered with flocks and the valleys are mantled with grain; help me to shout for joy and sing (Ps. 65:8, 13). For You care for me far more than the land You enrich abundantly. Flood my dry soul with the streams of God and fill me with joy (Ps. 65:9).

THE ABILITY TO BELIEVE GOD
DEVELOPS MOST OFTEN THROUGH
EXPERIENCE. FAITHFUL YESTERDAY,
HE WILL NOT BE UNFAITHFUL TODAY.

Lord God, help me to remember You when I go to bed. Occupy my thoughts through the watches of the night. Because You are my help, I sing in the shadow of Your wings. My soul clings to You; Your right hand upholds me (Ps. 63:6–8).

I know whom I have believed, and am convinced that You, Lord, are able to guard what I have entrusted to You (2 Tim. 1:12).

You are the One who hears prayer. To You may all men come! When I was overwhelmed by sins, You forgave my transgressions. Blessed are those You choose and bring near to live in Your courts! I am filled with the good things of Your house, of Your holy temple (Ps. 65:2–4).

SELF-MADE FORTRESSES NOT ONLY
KEEP LOVE FROM GOING OUT, THEY
KEEP LOVE FROM COMING IN. WE RISK
BECOMING CAPTIVES THERE.

Faithful, loving Lord, according to Your Word, two are better than one, because they have a good return for their work: if one falls down, his friend can help him up. But pity the man who falls and has no one to help him up! (Eccles. 4:9–10, 12).

Help me to form healthy relationships and find support in those who encourage me to get back on my feet and walk with You when I fall. Between You, me when I'm willing, and a good friend to hold me accountable, a cord of three strands is not quickly broken.

You warn us, "He who separates himself seeks his own desire; He quarrels against all sound wisdom" (Prov. 18:1, NASB). Help me to be very careful not to isolate myself.

CHRISTIANS CAN ONLY BE TRUE TO THEMSELVES WHEN THEY'RE DEMONSTRATING THAT THEY BELONG TO GOD.

Father, help me to have absolute assurance that I am a child of God, because the whole world system is presently under the control of the evil one (I John 5:19).

Lord, Your Word tells me not to believe every spirit, but to test the spirits to see whether they are from God, because many false prophets have gone out into the world (I John 4:1).

Please teach me how to follow this command accurately and effectively. Thank You for assuring me that because I am Your dear child, I have overcome all spirits not of God because the One who is in me is greater than the one who is in the world (I John 4:4).

HE BOUGHT US FROM SIN'S SLAVE
MASTER SO WE COULD EXPERIENCE
ABUNDANT LIFE. HE BOUGHT US
TO SET US FREE.

My Redeemer, I know that it was not with perishable things such as silver or gold that I was redeemed from the empty way of life handed down to me from my forefathers, but with the precious blood of Christ, a lamb without blemish or defect (1 Pet. 1:18–19).

Lord God, I know that my body is a temple of the Holy Spirit, who is in me, whom I have received from You. I am not my own; I was bought at a price. Therefore I desire to honor You with my body (1 Cor. 6:19–20).

And since I am a temple of Your Holy Spirit, I pray that You will cause Your glory to fill this temple of God like You did in days of old! (2 Chron. 5:14).

NO ONE IS MORE PLEASURABLE TO BE AROUND THAN A PERSON WHO HAS HAD HER CUP FILLED BY THE LORD JESUS CHRIST.

Lord, as a member of the body of Christ, help me consider how I may spur others on toward love and good deeds. I will not give up meeting with others in Christ, as some are in the habit of doing, but I choose to encourage others—and all the more as I see the Day approaching (Heb. 10:24–25).

I pray that I may also be active in sharing my faith, so that I will have a full understanding of every good thing I have in Christ (Philem. 6). Please help me to see that I cannot share something I don't have. I must possess faith to share it!

I have gained access by faith into this grace in which I now stand, and I rejoice in the hope of the glory of God (Rom. 5:2).

GOD CHANGES US FROM THE INSIDE OUT, RENEWING OUR MINDS, STARVING OUR SELFISH TENDENCIES, TEACHING US TO FORM NEW HABITS.

Lord, Your Spirit clearly says that in the later times some will abandon the faith and follow deceiving spirits and things taught by demons (I Tim. 4:I). Please help me to be very discerning of deceptive teaching. Help me never to abandon the faith to follow after a lie.

Father God, You want to present me holy in Your sight, without blemish and free from accusation, and You will do this if I continue in my faith, not moved from the hope held out in the gospel (Col. I:22–23).

I pray, too, that You will place others in my path who will continue with me for my progress and joy in the faith (Phil. I:25).

IN ALL THE CHANGES HE IS MAKING
WITHIN YOU AND ME, HE REJOICES
IN THE FEW THINGS THAT CALL FOR
BLESSED SAMENESS.

My wise and trustworthy God, according to Your Word, trials come to me so that my faith—of greater worth than gold, which perishes even though refined by fire—may be proved genuine and may result in praise, glory, and honor when Jesus Christ is revealed (1 Pet. 1:7).

Father, You have told me that the testing of my faith develops perseverance (James 1:3). Please help me to not refuse to be faithful in tests granted for my gain.

Help me, Lord, not to become weary in doing good, for at the proper time I will reap a harvest if I do not give up (Gal. 6:9).

Filling our minds with scripture acknowledging the "godship" of God is a crucial part of renewing our minds.

Father God, You command me for my own good not to merely listen to the Word but to do what it says. If I only listen and do not obey, I will undoubtedly deceive myself. Help me comprehend that the Word of God is my perfect law of liberty! (James 1:22; 1:25, KJV).

I praise You, God of heaven and Lord of earth! You are not a man, that You should lie, nor a son of man, that You should change Your mind. Do You speak and then not act? Do You promise and not fulfill? (Num. 23:19). You are always faithful, God! How grateful I am to know that You will never lie to me.

Your truth lives in me, O God, and will be with me forever (2 John 2).

JOY MAY SEEM TO PAUSE AS GRIEF
TAKES ITS COURSE, BUT THOSE WHOSE
BROKEN HEARTS ARE BOUND BY HIM
WILL EXPERIENCE IT AGAIN.

Jesus, Lord and Savior, help me to fight the good fight of the faith, taking hold of the eternal life to which I was called when I made my good confession in the presence of witnesses (1 Tim. 6:12).

O God, help me always to be thankful that I am loved by You, because from the beginning You chose me to be saved through the sanctifying work of the Spirit and through belief in the truth (2 Thess. 2:13).

You, O Lord, love me with an everlasting love; You have drawn me with loving kindness. You will build me up again and I will be rebuilt. I will take up my tambourine and go out to dance with the joyful! (Jer. 31:3–4).

HEALING BEGINS WHEN WE RECOGNIZE HOW VULNERABLE OUR EMPTY PLACES MAKE US AND SEEK WHOLENESS IN CHRIST ALONE.

I gratefully acknowledge that I have been crucified with You, Christ, and I no longer live, but You live in me. The life I live in the body, I live by faith in You, the Son of God; You love me and gave Yourself for me. I do not set aside the grace of God, for if righteousness could be gained through the law, You died for nothing! (Gal. 2:20–21).

You, Jesus Christ, are the faithful witness, the firstborn from the dead, the ruler of the kings of the earth. To You—who loves me and has freed me from my sins by Your blood, and has made me to be part of Your kingdom and priests to serve Your God and Father—to You be glory and power for ever and ever! Amen (Rev. 1:5–6).

THE REASON YOU DON'T HAVE
TO BUCKLE TO DISCOURAGEMENT
IS THE PRESENCE OF GOD IN THE
MIDDLE OF YOUR CIRCUMSTANCES.

Lord, many are the woes of the wicked, but Your unfailing love surrounds the one who trusts in You (Ps. 32:10). You are so trustworthy, God. Please help me to place my complete trust in You.

For in the day of trouble You will keep me safe in Your dwelling; You will hide me in the shelter of Your tabernacle and set me high upon a rock.

Then my head will be exalted above the enemies who surround me; at Your tabernacle will I sacrifice with shouts of joy; I will sing and make music to the Lord (Ps. 27:5–6). Your help to me is greater than life. Knowing that You are my defender gives me the strength to press ahead.

BE PATIENT AND GET TO KNOW HIM
THROUGH THE PROCESS OF HEALING.
YOU WILL SEE FRUIT. I PROMISE.
BETTER YET, HE PROMISES.

Because of Your great love for me, You, God, who are rich in mercy, made me alive with Christ even when I was dead in transgressions. It is by grace I have been saved (Eph. 2:4–5).

O Lord, I earnestly pray that I may live a life worthy of You and may please You in every way: bearing fruit in every good work, growing in the knowledge of God, being strengthened with all power according to Your glorious might so that I may have great endurance and patience, and joyfully giving thanks to the Father, who has qualified me to share in the inheritance of the saints in the kingdom of light (Col. 1:10–12).

GOD IS NEVER UNBIASED TOWARD
HIS CHILDREN. HE NEVER PARTS THE
SEA OF HIS FATHOMLESS LOVE TO
TAKE US ACROSS BEGRUDGINGLY.

Dear Lord, why am I always surprised at the painful trials I suffer, as though something strange were happening to me? Help me to rejoice that I participate in the sufferings of Christ, so that I may be overjoyed when Your glory is revealed (I Pet. 4:12–13).

For You have declared that You know the plans You have for me. Your plans are to prosper me and not to harm me, plans to give me hope and a future. Because of all You've done for me through Your Son, Jesus, when I call upon You and come and pray to You, You will listen. I will seek You and find You when I seek You with all my heart. You have declared, "I will be found by you." You will bring me back from captivity (Jer. 29:11–14).

GO AHEAD AND WASH A FEW FEET. GOD'S MOST LIBERATED SERVANTS ARE THOSE WHO KNOW THEY HAVE NOTHING ELSE TO PROVE.

O Father, Your Word calls me to the high pursuit of being an imitator of You, God. Therefore, as a dearly loved child, I am freed to live a life of love, just as Christ loved me and gave Himself up for me as a fragrant offering and sacrifice to You (Eph. 5:1).

You have shown me what is good. And what do You, Lord, require of me? To act justly and to love mercy and to walk humbly with my God (Mic. 6:8).

Yes, this is what You, the Lord Almighty, say: "Show mercy and compassion to one another." You have told me in my heart not to think evil of others (Zech. 7:9–10). Flood my heart with love for those You've placed in my life, even those who are difficult to love.

NO MATTER WHAT KIND OF REJECTION YOU MAY HAVE SUFFERED, PRAYING THE SCRIPTURE CAN BE USED BY GOD TO BRING YOU STRENGTH.

According to Your Word, blessed am I when men hate me, when they exclude me and insult me and reject my name as evil because of the Son of Man. I am to rejoice in that day and leap for joy, because great is my reward in heaven (Luke 6:22–23).

For at one time I too was foolish, disobedient, deceived and enslaved by all kinds of passions and pleasures. I lived in malice and envy, being hated and hating others (Titus 3:3). I acknowledge the misery of living outside of You.

Lord, I want it to be said of me that my many sins have been forgiven—for I have loved much. The person who has been forgiven little loves little (Luke 7:47).

THE LORD GOD OMNIPOTENT REIGNETH. HE IS GOD, AND THERE IS NO OTHER. WHEN HE STANDS TO HIS FEET, HIS ENEMIES ARE SCATTERED.

Lord Jesus, You have revealed to us that one day, You whose name is the Word of God will be dressed in a robe dipped in blood. The armies of heaven will follow you, riding on white horses and dressed in fine linen, white and clean.

Out of Your mouth will come a sharp sword with which to strike down the nations. You will rule them with an iron scepter. You will tread the winepress of the fury of the wrath of God Almighty. On Your robe and on Your thigh You have this name written: King of kings and Lord of lords (Rev. 19:13–16).

Yes, You are coming soon! Amen. Come, Lord Jesus! Until then, Your grace is with Your people (Rev. 22:20–21).

THE INFINITE, ETERNAL, OMNIPRESENT GOD WOOS TO HIS HEART THOSE WHO WILL DRAW NEAR TO HIM.

Lord, the Scripture declares that the whole world is a prisoner of sin, so that what was promised, being given through faith in Jesus Christ, might be given to those who believe (Gal. 3:22).

Those who oppose You will be shattered. You will thunder against them from heaven; You will judge the ends of the earth (1 Sam. 2:10). But those who know Your name will trust in You, for You, Lord, have never forsaken those who seek You (Ps. 9:10).

Lord God, help me draw near to You with a sincere heart in full assurance of faith, having my heart sprinkled to cleanse me from a guilty conscience and having my body washed with pure water (Heb. 10:22).

To know how best to bind up
the heart broken by betrayal,
Christ chose to experience it.
He ministers to us by example.

Father, since I have been justified through faith, I have peace with You through my Lord Jesus Christ (Rom. 5:1).

I praise You, my God, because I now have as a great high priest the One who has gone through the heavens, Jesus the Son of God! This allows me to hold firmly to the faith I profess! (Heb. 4:14).

Lord, according to Your wonderful Word, this is the victory that has overcome the world, even our faith. Who is it that overcomes the world? Only the one who believes that Jesus is the Son of God (1 John 5:4–5). Help me to see that faith is crucial if I am going to be a victor and an overcomer.

TRUSTING AN INVISIBLE GOD DOESN'T
COME NATURALLY TO US. IT GROWS
ONLY BY STEPPING OUT IN FAITH AND
MAKING THE CHOICE TO TRUST.

My God, You say to me in Your Word, "I,
even I, am he who comforts you" (Isa. 51:12).
Thank You, Lord! Help me to sense and respond to Your comfort.

Lord, You offer to rescue those who love
You and protect those who acknowledge Your
name. I will call upon You, and You will answer
me; You will be with me in trouble, You will
deliver me and honor me. Lord, I ask You to
satisfy me with long life and show me Your salvation (Ps. 91:14–16).

Heal me, and I will be healed; save me and
I will be saved, for You are the One I praise.
How I celebrate the fact that You have not run
away from being my shepherd; You have not
desired the day of despair (Jer. 17:14, 16).

CHRIST LONGS TO SEE THE LOVELY
FACE OF HIS BRIDE, HIS BELOVED.
AND HE WILL NOT BE DISAPPOINTED.
YOU WILL BE A BEAUTIFUL BRIDE.

Father God, Your Word exhorts me to sow for myself righteousness, reap the fruit of unfailing love, and break up my unplowed ground; for it is time to seek You, Lord, until You come to shower righteousness on me! (Hos. 10:12).

For my Maker is my husband—the Lord Almighty is Your name—the Holy One of Israel is my Redeemer; You are called the God of all the earth.

You will call me back as if I were a wife deserted and distressed in spirit—a wife who married young, only to be rejected. With deep compassion You will bring me back. You may chasten me, but with everlasting kindness You will have compassion on me (Isa. 54:5–8).

ASK GOD TO CAUSE HIS WORD TO ABIDE IN YOU AND BRING ITS PROPERTIES OF EFFERVESCENT LIFE, POWER, AND EFFECTIVENESS WITH IT.

O God, You are my God, earnestly I seek You; my soul thirsts for You, my body longs for You, in a dry and weary land where there is no water.

I have seen You in the sanctuary and beheld Your power and Your glory. Because Your love is better than life, my lips will glorify You. I will praise You as long as I live, and in Your name I will lift up my hands. My soul will be satisfied as with the richest of foods! (Ps. 63:1–5).

Help me, then, not to grieve, for Your joy is my strength (Neh. 8:10). If I call to You, You will answer me and tell me great and unsearchable things I do not know (Jer. 33:3).

Not only is a broken heart inevitable from time to time, it is one of the primary emotional rites of passage into maturity.

You, Lord, are close to the brokenhearted and save those who are crushed in spirit (Ps. 34:18). You are surely so close to me, Lord. Help me to sense Your presence in my life. I need You more than I need the next breath.

I am convinced that neither death nor life, neither angels nor demons, neither the present nor the future, nor any powers, neither height nor depth, nor anything else in all creation, will be able to separate me from Your love, O God, that is in Christ Jesus my Lord (Rom. 8:38–39).

Lord Jesus, I eagerly expect and hope that I will in no way be ashamed, but will have sufficient courage so that now as always Christ will be exalted (Phil. 1:20).

ONE OF THE PRIMARY REASONS GOD
SENT HIS SON TO EARTH WAS TO
BRING TENDER SALVE AND RELIEF TO
THOSE WHOSE HEARTS WERE BROKEN.

Father God, Your Word says that we were born in slavery under the basic principles of the world. But when the time had fully come, You sent Your Son, born of a woman, born under law, to redeem those of us who were under the law, so that we might receive the full rights of sons.

And because we are now sons of God through our faith and belief in the Incarnate Christ, You sent the Spirit of Your Son into our hearts, the Spirit who calls out, "Abba, Father."

So we are no longer slaves but are sons. And since we are sons, You have made us Your heirs also (Gal. 4:3–7). May I truly celebrate this divine gift of grace today.

THE DIVINE DILEMMA: TWO LOVES—
ONE FOR THE WORLD, ONE FOR HIS
ONLY SON. AND ONE DEMANDED THE
SACRIFICE OF THE OTHER.

Father, may my attitude be the same as that of Christ Jesus who, being in very nature God, did not consider equality with You a thing to be grasped, but made Himself nothing, taking the very nature of a servant, being made in human likeness.

And being found in appearance as a man, he humbled himself and became obedient to death—even death on a cross.

Therefore You highly exalted Him to the highest place and gave Him a name that is above every name, that at the name of Jesus every knee should bow, in heaven and on earth and under the earth, and every tongue confess that He is Lord, to Your glory and honor (Phil. 2:5–11). Hallelujah, praise Your name!

ONE OF THE MOST BEAUTIFUL ELEMENTS OF SALVATION IS ITS SIMPLICITY. CHRIST HAS ALREADY DONE ALL THE WORK ON THE CROSS.

My soul glorifies the Lord and my spirit rejoices in God my Savior (Luke 1:46–47).

Father, thank You for making me alive with Christ when I was dead in my sins and in the uncircumcision of my sinful nature. You forgave me all my sins, having canceled the written code, with its regulations, that was against me and that stood opposed to me. Christ took it away, nailing it to His cross. And having disarmed the powers and authorities, Christ Jesus made a public spectacle of them, triumphing over them by the cross (Col. 2:13–15).

Fill me with all joy and peace as I trust in You, so that I may overflow with hope by the power of the Holy Spirit (Rom. 15:13).

HE GIVES US A SUDDEN SPLASH OF
HAPPINESS HERE AND THERE SO WE
CAN WET OUR TOES IN WHAT WE'LL
BE SWIMMING IN FOR ETERNITY.

Lord God, Your Word says, "The people walking in darkness have seen a great light; on those living in the land of the shadow of death a light has dawned" (Isa. 9:2).

I pray that the eyes of my heart may be enlightened in order that I may know the hope to which You have called me, the riches of Your glorious inheritance in the saints, and Your incomparably great power for us who believe (Eph. 1:18–19).

Lord Jesus Christ, may You and God my Father, who loves me and by His grace gave me eternal encouragement and good hope, encourage my heart and strengthen me in every good deed and word (2 Thess. 2:16–17).

THE THOUGHT OF THE FUTURE
OF THE UNREDEEMED SHOULD
MAKE US SHIVER. WE SHOULD
PRAY FOR ALL TO REPENT.

According to Your Word, the god of this age has blinded the minds of unbelievers, so that they cannot see the light of the gospel of the glory of Christ, the image of God (2 Cor. 4:4). Your Word also says that only in Christ is the veil removed (2 Cor. 3:14). Please cause my lost loved ones to turn to You so that the veil will be taken away (2 Cor. 3:16).

Lord, I thank You for the assurance that my enemy and accuser is a defeated foe. He will be judged for all his deception, wickedness, perversion, and lust to see people lost and tormented. The devil, who has deceived so many, will be thrown into the lake of burning sulfur where he will be tormented day and night forever and ever (Rev. 20:10).

ETERNITY CAN BE
WELL SECURED EVEN WHILE
LIFE ON EARTH REMAINS
SHAKY AT BEST.

Lord God, according to Your Word much woe has come to the earth and the sea because the devil has come down to us. He is filled with fury because he knows his time is short (Rev. 12:12).

How I look forward to an eternity void of the kingdom of darkness. No longer will there be any curse. The throne of God and of the Lamb will be in the city, and Your servants will serve You. We will see Your face, and Your name will be on our foreheads.

There will be no more night. We will not need the light of a lamp or the light of the sun, for You will give us light. And we will enjoy Your reign forever and ever (Rev. 22:3–5).

CHRIST'S PEACE HAS ALREADY BEEN
GIVEN TO US IF WE HAVE RECEIVED
HIM. WE JUST DON'T ALWAYS KNOW
HOW TO ACTIVATE IT.

Glorious God, I thank You for qualifying me to share in the inheritance of the saints in the kingdom of light. For You have rescued me from the dominion of darkness and brought me into the kingdom of the Son You love, in whom I have redemption, the forgiveness of sins (Col. 1:12–14).

My Father, please help me always know You are near and not to be anxious about anything, but in everything, by prayer and petition, with thanksgiving, to present my requests to You.

If I do, Your peace, which transcends all understanding, will guard my heart and mind in Christ Jesus.

BELIEVE GOD FOR EVERY PROMISE
INTENDED FOR THE SOIL OF EARTH,
AND PERSEVERE FAITHFULLY UNTIL
THE FULL INHERITANCE OF HEAVEN.

Lord God, You have said that Your righteous one will live by faith and if he shrinks back You will not be pleased with him (Heb. 10:38).

Lord, I want to live a life that is pleasing to You. The life that pleases you is also a life that You so readily bless (Heb. 11:6). I don't want to miss the great adventures You mapped out for me by shrinking back from a walk of faith.

O God, more than anything, I want to finish the race one of these days and be able to say, "I have kept the faith." If I keep the faith, You will have a crown of righteousness waiting for me! (2 Tim. 4:7–8).